Wags to You
Short and Long Dog Tails

Clark L. Roberts

Insight Publishing
Sevierville, TN

Wags to You - Short and Long Dog Tails ©2014
By Clark L. Roberts
ISBN: 978-1-62452-024-2
Insight Publishing
Cover Design: Steve Wilson
Formatting and Layout: Chris Ott

ENDORSEMENTS

I met Clark in 1993 when I sought out a successful blind person to learn from due to my quickly losing vision at age 53. Clark, impressively, was a blind skier as well as having ridden in the STP (Seattle to Portland Bicycle Classic). He insisted that I bring my wife and our two young daughters to his home so that we, as a family, could meet him and his dog guide to experience blindness in action. We did this and cemented a long-term relationship that is ongoing. Clark was a huge help in my transition. He is real; he cares, and is a great man of courage! There is much more I could say; however, this book will help you learn much of what I love and respect in this fine, Christ-centered man.

In Jesus Christ,
Kimball Holt Dunbar

Clark is a real "make lemonade" kind of guy. Any time spent in getting to know him and his passage through life is an investment in your own better perspective.

Mark O'Neill, cancer survivor and high school youth worker.
Orcas Island, WA

Surrounded in a world of darkness, Clark Roberts paints a brilliant picture of how vibrant life can be if we only overcome the self-imposed barriers that hold us back. Blindness has not stopped him from living the same exciting life he encourages others to embrace. Whether it's speaking or cycling, Clark uses the most powerful form of communication of all...example.

Eric Miller, Founder/President of Rush-Miller Foundation

As a part of my job, I get the pleasure of meeting people from all walks of life. Occasionally, someone like Clark comes along and etches himself into your memory. It is the people who have a thirst for life, and not only strive to quench their own thirst but walk others hand-in-hand to the watering hole who leave an indelible mark. We need more Clarks around this world, helping others see what is possible and achieving their goals.

Jordan McElderry
Skydive Snohomish

REVIEWS

Wags to You: Short and Long Dog Tails is an authentic, well-written collection of stories that will touch and amuse any person who has ever had the privilege of experiencing the power of the human-canine partnership. Whether you are a pet owner, a member of a guide dog team, or wondering if the guide dog lifestyle is for you, Mr. Roberts' stories will strike a chord with you. They will capture your imagination, your heart, and tickle your funny bone. His stories, and the stories he has collected from other guide dog users, underscore the amazing ability of guide dogs to bring out the best in their handlers, their handlers' families, and in the larger community. I found myself laughing and crying in equal measure. In the end, I was happy to have read *Wags to You* and happier still that Mr. Roberts is an alumnus of Guide Dogs for the Blind and has chosen to share his story and the stories of his friends.

Karen Woon
Senior Marketing Manager
Guide Dogs for the Blind

This sweet book tells the story of a man who did not want to accept his blindness at first due to his love of all things outdoors and his need to stay active. We get to hear about the adventures of finding the right guide dog and all the amazing people you get to meet when you accept the responsibility of a guide dog. There are also heartwarming stories of other people and their furry companions.

This book is a good one to curl up with and lose yourself in the story. It is a quick read and does not take a lot of thought but will grab you if you are a dog lover. It is a book that you can read quickly or just a chapter at a time and come back to it with no problem. I would recommend this to any dog lover!

Lisa Steckler
Dog About Town

TABLE OF CONTENTS

FOREWORD

"WAGS TO YOU" IS A MUST READ for anyone who wants to know more about blind people and/or blindness, has a dog, or is interested in learning more about dogs. I have been using guide dogs for 50 years and have worked with seven dogs through my life. These wonderful dogs have been with me in good times and challenging times, including my escape from the World Trade Center on 9-11. I wrote about my experiences in *Thunder Dog* and *Running With Roselle* but, even so, *Wags To You* kept me enthralled right from page one.

Clark has done a masterful job of describing his experiences and gives an incredible view into what it was like when he was losing his eyesight. His book draws in the reader and you feel like you are living every moment not only with him, but with all the others whose dogs he includes in his story. He weaves a great tale that educates, entertains, and shows firsthand how each of us can do more than we ever thought possible.

Clark also gives wonderful insights into the life of Guide Dogs for the Blind puppy raisers—those wonderful people who transform the lives of the puppies and prepare them to be trained for guide work.

You will not be disappointed with *Wags For You*. I hope you enjoy it as much as I have. Like me, you will read it again and again.

Michael Hingson
www.michaelhingson.com
The Michael Hingson Group, INC.

INTRODUCTION

Close your eyes and imagine that all of your hopes, dreams and desires are in front of you—everything that you enjoy—sports, music, hobbies, business, a full life. Then a doctor steps in and announces that in 15-20 years you will lose your sight, go blind. Nothing you do can alter the course; you have a choice to make—accept or reject the new reality. What do you do?

My name is Clark Roberts and this was where I found myself as a freshman in college at the age of 18. I was excited and ready to be on my own, looking forward to a life full of new friends, new adventures and new opportunities. Going blind was not a part of my plan and I was devastated; it felt like I had been betrayed by God. I wanted to reject the news; at one point I was so low that I thought of ending it all—check out, be done with life. Fortunately I held on; I knew God had a plan for me, a plan not to harm me but to prosper me, a plan to give me hope and a future. (Jeremiah 29:11)

When you are walking through the challenges of life, it's easy to put up walls: walls of denial, self-doubt, walls of despair. During those moments you need to remember that God has a very special purpose for you, that your life is a gift. In the beginning this was difficult for me since I did not want this new "gift" this "gift of blindness." I thought initially that the doctors had messed up. Then the reality hit me and I was scared. I didn't know how to function and did not want assistance from anyone.

During that time I was not a very nice person to be around but I was blessed with a loving family; one that supported me through the good times and the difficult times. My parents had raised me and my three siblings in a strong Christian home—one where we were shown early in life that no matter what our circumstances, there was no giving up, no quitting, no bailing out. They reminded me that God had a plan for me. Eventually I realized that by trusting others and allowing them to support me and to encourage me that I, in turn, could encourage them. But trust was one of the things I had to learn to give again.

Through my journey I learned to trust—and thanks to amazing people and my five amazing guide dogs, trust is now something that I interact with daily. You see, TRUST means to To Rely Upon Someone or Something Totally. First I had to learn how to completely trust God with this new life, a life that was now in physical darkness. Next I had to trust myself and my ability to live a full life, and lastly I had to trust those around me.

Today I can look back and know that my sight loss gave me opportunities that I never would have imagined. If I had rejected the news and the "gift of blindness," I would have missed out on all of the incredible blessings God has given me. I have found freedom of mobility through five amazing guide dogs, I have connected with thousands of people and been blessed by people that I have met through this journey. As you read the following pages, remember this. You were created for a specific purpose that only you can fulfill and that your life is a gift; unwrap it, cherish it and live your life in a way that challenges others to live their life in a new way.

-Clark Roberts

CHAPTER ONE
Receiving the News

RECEIVING THE NEWS

Winter, a glorious time in the Pacific Northwest when Mother Nature covers the earth with all of her glorious beauty; white fluffy snow blanketed the land and frost glittered along the river banks, framing the rocks and trees. I was an 18-year-old freshman and had just awakened from a restless night. My mind was preoccupied as I was preparing to go to an eye doctor's appointment to review some test results. These were a follow-up from an appointment I had two weeks prior. I moved as if I was in slow motion, each step heavy as I contemplated what the doctor could possibly want to discuss with me.

Exiting the dorm that morning, I was met by a cold wind blowing out of the north; the brisk air lifted my spirits and erased the heaviness of the morning. The crust of the snow gave way like a crisp cracker, crunching loudly with each step. Laughing and talking on my way to class, I would watch my breath trail off into the atmosphere. I stopped to watch a couple of squirrels playing in the snow and above me I could see birds perched on icy telephone wires. It seemed I was not the only one enjoying the cold winter day, as students around me were engaging in a quick snowball fight. I was jarred back to reality by a buddy asking me, "Clark, are you going to class today?" Realizing I was standing in front of the building where my first class was, I decided I should enter. Sitting in Animal Science class, my mind wandered from current information about livestock breeds, economic forecasting, and crop prices to trying to guess what I would learn later that afternoon regarding the eye tests.

Before I knew it, class was over and I headed back to the dorm, dropped my books, went to lunch and then decided to hang out with my buddies and wait. Waiting quickly became the theme of the day. I woke up and waited, waited for class to start, waited for class to get over, waited for the day to pass, and then waited to drive to Pullman from Moscow.

Upon entering the doctor's office, I would wait and then wait some more before he entered to go over the results. My eyes scanned the walls; I remember seeing wildlife photos along with diplomas from medical school, and documents stating that in the State of Washington he was legal to practice his trade. Again my mind began to wander: What would this appointment bring? What I would learn? What news did the doctor have for me? Once again I would hear my name and be jarred back to reality as the doctor entered and, with a resounding "thump," placed a thick folder on his desk. He engaged me in some small talk and then stated that he had some news for me. Internally I am thinking, "Okay, so you have some news, so let's get on with this." "Clark" he said, "I have looked at the results every way I can and I keep coming up with the same information." Feeling my insides screaming, I wanted to explode with "What are the results?" His next words made my head reel: "You have retinitis pigmentosa (aka "RP") and you are going blind."

The room began spinning and I heard myself ask, "What did you say?" Again he stated; "Clark, you have retinitis pigmentosa and within fifteen to eighteen years you will be totally blind." In that moment my entire world stopped. I heard my heart beating loudly. Somewhere in the room I recognized the doctor's voice speaking as if from a mile away. Slowly his voice came back into focus. Over the next forty-five minutes I listened—but I didn't listen because I didn't want to listen. My brain had shut down, my emotions were like a pendulum swinging from total sorrow to uncontrollable anger, and I came apart emotionally.

As I sat there feeling like my life had just been swept out to sea, the doctor leaned in and said, "Clark, I don't like the way you are receiving the news." I could not believe how unfeeling a person could be when they had just dumped your life on the floor and scattered it in the wind. What was I supposed to do, jump up and down, run around his desk shouting, "Hurrah, I'm going to be blind?"

Leaving the doctor's office, my brain was numb. Disconnected thoughts ran through my head. What would I do, what should I do, and could I even do anything? At that time in my life all I knew about blind people was that they didn't have much of a life. They would sit on street corners and sell light bulbs, make brooms and put erasers on the end of pencils. No thank you, I did not want that kind of life.

Arriving back at my dorm, I dragged myself up three flights of stairs just to enter a dark empty room. Tearing my coat off, I threw it across the room and collapsed on the floor, crying like a baby. In that moment my world was covered in darkness and my thoughts gave way to it; a voice inside me whispered, "Check out, be done with the pain, be done with life."

In the hours that followed I fought through the darkness and held on tightly to my belief that God had a plan for me. A knock on my door and a voice from the hall told me that my parents were on the phone. There I was, standing alone in the middle of the dorm hallway, leaning into the wall, crying with my parents. I ached to feel their arms holding me close, to hear them tell me it would be okay, to wake up and realize I had been having a terrible nightmare.

I had been asked to return to the doctor's office to be examined by a specialist. The thought of having them poke and prod my eyes did not excite me. The specialist was going to determine how far the disease had progressed and if it would naturally arrest itself. This was encouraging but still left me uncertain.

Leaving the doctor's office, I returned to life on campus. I was uncertain that my friends would accept me with blindness labeling my future. Not knowing when my sight loss would be complete, I kept quiet about the appointment. The news from the previous day had left me confused, numb, and full of questions. Blindness—what was I supposed to do with this? Before receiving this news I had a plan for my life; now it had been rearranged—I no longer knew if I was actually going to have a life.

Over the next few weeks I tried to go about life as normal—even my roommate Scott did not know what was happening to me. Being roommates, he noticed that something was wrong and we danced around this issue for two weeks until he ambushed me on a Friday night. We went to A&W to eat dinner and while there he dropped a question: "Clark, what's up in your life and why are you acting like you are?" Gulping down my food and trying not to choke, I stared at him for a few seconds. "Scott, what do you know about retinitis Pigmentosa?" Scott's answer mirrored what I had been told two weeks before and he asked, "Why?" My eyes filled with tears as I told him that I had been diagnosed with this disease. Pent-up emotion released itself and over the next few hours he and I talked and cried. Scott said, "Clark, no matter what, you are my friend and I am here for you." Those were the words I needed to hear.

It was then that I began to take steps towards understanding what was going to happen. I knew that God had a plan for me and I held on to that knowledge during the days, weeks, and months that followed.

MOVING FORWARD

Not long after my diagnosis, I began meeting with a Rehabilitation Counselor from the Commission for the Blind. The counselor wanted me to enter a training program that would teach me life skills and provide me with tools to adapt to a life without sight. During this time, my college grades suffered and I was notified that I had been academically disqualified and could not return for at least one semester. I told my counselor that I would not even look at entering the training program until that fall. I didn't care about anything and decided the best course for the summer was to play.

One afternoon I was sitting in my bedroom, sunshine warming my face as it danced through the window. I had just received the latest edition of Western Horsemen magazine and I was eager to read the articles. Sitting at my desk, I began to go through the magazine from cover to cover enjoying the pictures of well-bred quarter horses and headlines of articles that interested me. As I proceeded to read, I landed upon an article that was of particular interest to me. It wasn't long before I realized that I was reading and rereading the same sentence. My eyes would track across the sentence and, as they came back to the beginning, I found myself not being able to find the next sentence. In that moment, I knew in my heart that the blindness was not going to arrest itself, and I knew it was not going to take fifteen years. I was scared by the knowledge that my world was literally going to fade to black.

Waking the next morning, I stood in front of the mirror and asked myself a question. "Clark, if you wake up tomorrow and it is all gone, will you be ready to interact with life?" I had no choice but to be honest and answer with a resounding "NO!" I either had to humble myself, swallow my pride, and learn how to live this life or it was going to capture me and hold me hostage for the rest of my life. Not long after this I contacted my counselor and told her that I would be ready to enter the training program in September. I may have been dragging my heels the entire way; I entered the program not knowing what I would learn, but I was willing to step out in faith and try.

That summer I spent every moment living life and making memories. I wanted to catalog everything both visually and mentally. I went water skiing, backpacking, camping, and horseback riding. I memorized the beauty of every sunrise and sunset I could take in. I did everything that allowed me to be outside and distracted me from what was coming. As dusk fell over the surrounding land and darkness fell over my eyes, I felt the fear creeping in. I did not know how to deal with the impending darkness and was concerned that maybe one day the light would not return when morning came. I heard a voice say to me, "Clark, no matter how dark your world gets, I am always here with you."

In the fall, I entered the orientation program at the Commission for the Blind and was introduced to some practical life skills, including Braille and the use of the white cane. At age nineteen I was trying to learn to read again, but this time in Braille, a communication system that allows one to read by feeling bumps in a pattern. I felt like I was back in the first grade starting all over again and I wanted nothing more than to take the books and flush them down the toilet.

The white cane did not make me feel any better about learning these tools as the cane and I did not see eye to eye. I remember thinking, even then, that there had to be a better tool for mobility. I reluctantly learned the basics of both Braille and the maneuvering of cane travel, but as soon as I left the training facility I stood the cane in the corner and threw the Braille books out the window. With sight loss looming closer each day, I was not ready to let go of my sighted world; my freedom, my choices, my dreams, and my desires. Life as I knew it was rapidly changing and I was doing my best to change with it.

CHAPTER TWO
Living the Dream

RUSTY AND SHEBA

About four years after learning that I was losing my eyesight I came face to face with reality. My visual acuity was diminishing, making it difficult for me to do many things. This day was especially taxing as I was sitting in my bedroom reading the classified ads in the *Western Horseman* magazine. As I attempted to read the magazine, the words would fade in and out. At this exact moment, emotion hit me as my mind could no longer hide the truth from my heart. With a sick feeling in my stomach, I realized what others had already been seeing. My sight was going fast and there was nothing I could do about it. This was a significant moment for me, and all I wanted to do was to keep my life as normal as possible.

For me, that meant trying to live my dream of working with the livestock industry before I lost my sight. I wanted to stay connected to that dream and had this idea to raise Australian Shepherds and sell them to cattle and sheep ranchers. As I was reading the magazine, I came across an advertisement from people that were selling puppies. I decided to go for it and purchased two Australian Shepherds. I received Sheba first. She was stocky and looked like a little polar bear. Her coloring was Blue Merle with a white forehead and white all the way through her nose. She had black and copper around her eyes, making her look like she was wearing dark sunglasses. Blue Merle is a bluish-grey color that darkens as the animal grows.

Two months later I received Rusty, my male. Rusty was a bit sleeker in stature and his color was Red Merle. When I received him at ten weeks old he looked a bit splotchy with dirty brick-red spots. As he grew, his color darkened and eventually covered his body in a gorgeous deep red, all except his front legs and a white stripe down the middle of his nose. I had the beginnings of my breeding stock.

Sheba and Rusty at 10 weeks

I remember wondering during that first year how this dream was going to play out. As I worked with both dogs, training them and enjoying them, it became more important to me to catalog every bit of how they looked, moved, played and interacted. While doing this I would watch their body language, noticing how both stood, cocking their heads to one side, their facial expressions saying, "Play with me." Watching them brought me such joy but, as we moved toward fall, the days got shorter and dusk came earlier, making it harder for me to see them. I was always grateful when morning came as it gave me another chance to see my dream in the light of day.

A DAY IN THE DESERT

One spring morning I was sitting on my bed watching the sun filtering through my bedroom window. Knowing that one day I would not have my sight, I found myself watching it move brightly across my room. I was mesmerized by the floating flecks of dust that seemed to flicker like small lightening bugs dancing on the incoming ray of sunlight. The air outside would be cool, but I knew that once the sun rose higher in the sky the temperature would also rise. This would be a beautiful day for a horseback ride. Getting out of bed, there was the aroma of coffee wafting throughout the house and the smell of breakfast cooking. When I entered the kitchen, I was met by an energetic Rusty and Sheba. Once fed and watered, they were ready to go and play.

I settled in with a cup of coffee and began to consider my options for the day. The telephone's ringing jolted me out of my reverie. My friend Newel was on the other end asking me if I had any plans for the day. I was not surprised when he suggested we go horseback riding on the Snake River in the Owyhee Desert. Newell arrived early that afternoon with his truck, trailer, riding gear, and two quarter horses already loaded and ready to go. Just as I was exiting the door, he called out to me suggesting that I bring the dogs. Rusty and Sheba eagerly hopped in the truck, ready for an adventure. Rusty worked his way immediately onto the seat between Newell and me, where Sheba normally would sit. Rusty always had a way of making sure he was a step ahead of Sheba. Sheba, being the lady that she was, jumped in and settled on the floor next to my feet. She knew she would have an opportunity to get Rusty back later. With the sun shining through the window as we drove, we shared stories about horses, life, and of course, dogs. It did not take us long to reach the Snake River; soon the truck was rattling down the gravel road, kicking up dust and rolling to a jolting stop.

Both Rusty and Sheba jumped out when the door opened, racing around like a couple of young puppies. The dogs could sense that an adventure was just moments away and they couldn't wait for us to get the horses out. Leaving the truck, we walked the horses down the road, crossed over the cattle guard and swung into the saddle. We began galloping down the river with the dogs running in front of us along the sagebrush-covered land.

As we rode we would watch the dogs running ahead of us—when suddenly we would lose sight of them, then see a puff of dust rise into the air. The dogs would take off running again, disappear, and we would see another puff of dust in the distance. This continued on and off over the next few miles. Curious, but never quite able to catch up to the adventurous dogs, we continued our ride. After a few miles, Rusty and Sheba were getting tired and we caught up to them. We then discovered that each time the dogs disappeared, they had fallen into badger holes that were hidden by the sagebrush. You would think that after falling into the first two or three, they would have learned to avoid them.

After completing our ride and watching these two Aussies dust themselves off, it was time to load the truck and head for home. Both dogs flopped into the truck, exhausted and dirty. This time Sheba held her own and got to ride shotgun while Rusty took the floor. They curled up in the sunshine and slept happily all the way home. Every now and then, their legs would flail like they were running and they would yip in their sleep. I am certain they were dreaming of chasing badgers in the Owyhee Desert.

THE BIG SKY COUNTRY

I am always amazed, even though I should not be, when God puts the pieces of your life together in a way you don't expect. When I purchased Rusty and Sheba, the intention and the dream was to breed stock dogs for ranchers. I knew the best market for selling stock dogs would be Montana, Wyoming and surrounding states. In the fall of 1976, my father announced that he had accepted a job in Missoula, Montana and we were moving! Within a few months of moving to Missoula, Sheba had her first litter of puppies. As the day approached for Sheba to give birth there was a feeling of excitement mixed with apprehension. What happens if I don't see all of the puppies she delivers? What happens if she needs help and I can't give it? With these questions in the back of my mind, I set up the birthing area for her in the basement of our home.

I watched amazed as Sheba delivered each puppy, carefully cleaning the tiny wet puppy, nurturing it, helping it to find a nipple to nurse on. If the puppy was too weak, she would push it away and not allow the puppy to nurse. Sheba's first litter consisted of thirteen puppies, but she only had ten nipples. One little puppy did not make it and two were too weak to continue. Sheba knew this and we allowed the miracle of birth and the mercy of death to take place. As all ten puppies nuzzled into Sheba, each searching for a place to nurse, she stood up to stretch. I chuckled as I looked at her—all engorged with milk, she looked like a walking milk truck.

My mom holding two of Sheba's puppies

Tail-Docking Time

14

THE HERDING GAME

Herding dogs have a natural instinct and desire to herd. They will naturally nip at the heads and heels of other animals, trying to redirect their paths. After Rusty and Sheba had their first litter of ten puppies, I quickly realized that this herding ability was a trait woven into the fiber of each puppy.

At about four weeks old, the puppies would begin playing what I liked to call the "herding game." With ten puppies in the "herd," they would play all day long. To start the game, they would decide among themselves who was going to be the herder and the rest of the litter would fall in behind as the herd. Playtime consisted of nipping at each other's heels; jumping over each other's backs and barking at the heads of the puppies that were in the herd. When the herder became weary he would fall out and become a part of the herd, at which time another pup would take the lead as the herder. This cycle would continue again and again and again until, exhausted and extremely content, they would crawl over each other and fall asleep in a puppy pile under the Montana sky. To this day, this is one of my most cherished visual memories.

THE DANCE AT DINNER

Feeding ten puppies at a time can regularly get quite crazy and comical. I would separate the puppies by feeding them from three bowls and they would all eat at the same time. It was like watching a physical comedy routine when they began to do what I call "pinwheel" eating.

Australian Shepherds - Feeding time: only two, but still fun to watch

I would set all three bowls on the ground and the puppies would pick a group and the group would pick a bowl. Each puppy would take a spot on the edge of the bowl and grab a mouth full of food and begin chewing. The circle of puppies around each bowl would then move to the left or right, depending on whatever direction was decided by the pups. As they were eating, they would continue rotating around in a pinwheel formation until all of the food in their bowl was gone. At that time, the puppies that had finished would move to the next bowl and crowd in on the other circle of puppies still eating. Three became six, six became nine...wait! don't forget about number ten! Shoving, squirming, wiggling, tails wagging, mouths full of food, they continued circling their new bowl in a well-choreographed dance until all the food was gone. I have to admit this type of pinwheel feeding with the Australian Shepherds is another one of those fantastic visual memories that still makes me laugh, even after all these years.

Clark, his brother James, Rusty, and two pups enjoy the sun

FADE TO BLACK

As I watched the puppies, I closed my eyes and wondered where each would end up? Would they make a great dog for a rancher or would they become a family pet? I opened my eyes to the sun beginning to set in the Montana sky. By the time they were nine weeks old, I had sold each one to homes and ranches in eastern Idaho, across Montana and even one to North Dakota. It was not easy letting them go, but it was an extension of my trying to stay connected and it was a part of my dream. I was satisfied to know that the puppies would one day help these ranchers by running herd on their livestock.

Then Sheba had her second litter of pups. When this litter was whelped, I soon realized that there were three tri-colored pups, two Blue Merles with copper and tan, and three solid red puppies that looked like little Hereford bulls. Again I would sit and watch the puppies play the herding game in the Montana sun, but with each day my ability to see them was deteriorating. I could no longer see their body shape unless the sun was shining just right. I could hear them running and playing but if they stood against the fence they would blend in, a perfect camouflage of color. I was desperate to hang onto my dream but was uncertain as to how long I could keep on.

Sheba had her third and smallest litter about two years after our journey together had begun. I tried my best to watch with my eyes but the retinitis pigmentosa had almost fully run its course. I changed the way I was looking at the puppies and began spending more time seeing their body shape during grooming time. I would take my hands and work them over their legs, backs and head, memorizing each of them as my eyes continued to weaken.

It was not long after their third litter that I noticed Rusty had a lump on his neck. After a couple of days it had not gone away so we took a trip to the veterinarian. My heart sank and tears filled my eyes as the doctor announced that Rusty had cancer of the lymph nodes—lymphatic sarcoma. Within a week I was back at the animal hospital putting him down. This disease had taken his life.

Sheba seemed to mourn the loss of Rusty, her mate, her companion, her play buddy. She slowed down and went into a depression a few months after Rusty had been put down. As I was returning from a friend's wedding in eastern Montana, my dad told me that Sheba was not doing well. As I ran my hands over her, examining every inch of her body I realized that she had a large mass similar in size and feel to when she was full of milk. But Sheba was not pregnant, so once again we were off to the vet. This time the veterinarian informed me she had cancer of her uterus. I took Sheba home with me and stayed close to her for the next two days; she slept most of the time and I slept right by her side. I knew what was coming but I was not ready to let her go. Sheba passed away at home with her head in my lap and with me stroking her head as I saw her for the last time. I was heartbroken; my beautiful Aussies were gone.

That afternoon, I sat out on the porch thinking about how two little Australian Shepherd puppies had impacted my life. The two plus years that I had with them, playing with them, racing around the yard, training them, breeding them, and watching the miracle of birth and the circle of life. I was blessed. God had given me a chance to live my dream and Rusty and Sheba had brought that dream to life. As I gazed out toward the fence, I could see there was no movement, no blurred images of puppies or dogs; just a fenced-in area that held nothing but my memories.

As I stood looking out, the sun began to set over my shoulder and everything became blurred. It was difficult to distinguish between the grass, the fence, and the tree line. The only details I had were those I had cataloged in my mind and etched deeply into my heart and soul. Not only had I lost both of my dogs to cancer, but my dream, like the end of a well-rehearsed play, had come to an end—curtain down, fade to black. On the horizon the darkness enveloped the Montana sky and, unknown to me, the darkness was about to overtake my life too — within a few months my eyesight would be gone.

CHAPTER THREE
Tools of the Trade

THE CANE

Tap, tap, tap.... I was so tired of that sound; the cane, the white cane. When my sight loss was first diagnosed I started learning how to use the white cane. In the beginning of my journey it was me and it was the cane; a recognized symbol of mobility, a tool for the visually impaired. I remember when my dad handed me my first collapsible cane as a gift. I wanted nothing to do with it and I threw it back in his face. As far as I was concerned, the cane was cold and inanimate with no warmth of companionship, no way to build a relationship of trust. I was supposed to rely upon this object and upon myself to get me from point A to point B safely—just the cane and me. All of this sounded logical, but when you are in denial, logic does not come into play.

When the retinitis pigmentosa took my sight in Montana, I could no longer avoid using the tools that I had been trained to use. The doctor had stated almost six years ago, that my blindness would happen in fifteen to eighteen years. I now knew that was not the case. In the beginning I attempted to live my life without the tools that I had been given, but eventually I just gave in. Each and every time I ventured out I would fight to arrive at my destination. Obstacles and every day roadblocks, which for a sighted person would be nothing, became a battle for me. This was a battle that I would lose every time, sometimes walking away bloody and bruised. Once again, the cane had gotten stuck in the crack of a sidewalk, jammed up against the bumper of a vehicle, or missed a lamp pole—causing me to find it with my forehead—car doors half open that the cane would miss and my chest would find. So there I was, frustrated, discouraged, and in pain!

As I settled into my life without sight, I used the tool of the cane and it showed the wear and tear of that use. As bruised as I would get, the cane also was bruised, bent and broken. I walked everywhere and I would jam the cane into a crack in the sidewalk; it would then jab me in the belly and bend at the joints. Eventually my cane would snap in two, and I wondered how on earth I was going to make it home. For the next six years I went through a cane each year, sometimes two, depending on how hard I worked the cane. Now, you might be asking yourself if there might have been a small amount of user error; possibly, but come on...there had to be a better, more freeing tool for mobility and I was eager to find it.

THE DOG, THE FRIEND, THE COMPANION

In June of 1985, at age 31, I met a woman who was using a guide dog from an organization called Leader Dogs for the Blind out of Michigan. She also told me of another school located in California, a different organization named Guide Dogs for the Blind, and I was intrigued. As I spent time with her, she described how she and the dog cohesively moved in and out of traffic, crossing streets and accomplishing the task of getting from point A to point B as a team. She would arrive at her destination much less frustrated than I, less discouraged and yes ... little to no blood. After walking alongside of her and her dog, I decided that this was something to pursue. My step was lighter as I realized that maybe there was a better tool for mobility!

I contacted both schools and was informed that after I submitted an application I would be screened to see if this would be a good fit for me. I filled out the application and sent it off to both organizations, and waited. I was accepted at both; the difference between them was a six-month wait for Guide Dogs for the Blind in California versus being able to go to Leader Dogs in September. I immediately made plans to fly to Michigan. During the plane ride from Seattle to Detroit, I had lots of time to think. I wondered if I would be able to do this. Could I trust enough to let go of the cane and take hold of the leash?

Once in Detroit, I proceeded to the campus where I would spend the next twenty-eight days training and getting to know my new dog. It's hard to describe the time that I was in Detroit. There was never a feeling of connection. I was matched with a black Labrador named Toby. Toby and I got along okay but it wasn't great and it wasn't smooth. After we had been home for two months, Toby growled at me when I stepped over him. My head jerked back and my heart skipped a beat. A dog that growls at its owner is only a step away from biting either its owner or, even worse, another person. I made the decision to return him.

I was not ready to give up, not yet. I knew that I had found something that for me was a better tool than the cane. So, determined to try again, I immediately put in a phone call to Guide Dogs for the Blind and asked if my application was still valid. It was and I booked my flight. The day came and I headed to the airport.

During the short flight, my mind was spinning with questions: Would this work this time? Would it be better? Could I do this again? Would this dog accept me and work efficiently for me? What kind of dog would it be? Would we get along? All of these questions and so many more would be answered as I continued on this trip.

I arrived at the campus that I would call "home" for the next twenty-eight days. Immediately I noticed a difference. Upon arriving you are oriented to the room and the dormitory building where you will live and interact with students from across the country. For the next two days I spent time with the other students and with Juno. Juno was the imaginary guide dog that each student would learn to work with, giving commands and being evaluated on their performance. This evaluation then helped the instructors with the final matching of dog to individual.

I will never forget that day—the Wednesday before Easter—it was D-Day. D-Day is Dog Day at Guide Dogs for the Blind, and on this particular day I would meet my first working Guide Dog.

When they brought my dog to me I felt a welling up of emotion. Grief came flooding back as I realized how much I had denied the impact of my sight loss on my life. As the tears flooded my eyes and slowly trailed down my cheeks, I realized again that I was not completely over the loss. I also realized the depth of this gift that I was about to receive, a gift of freedom. I picked up the leash, ran my hands down to the end of it and began working them quickly over my guide dog. From the top of her head to the tip of her tail, I began "seeing" my dog for the first time. We spent that evening sitting on the floor getting to know each other, connecting to each other, bonding and forming a team.

Early the next morning I was told that our class would take our first walk with our four-legged friends. As I sat waiting my turn I felt a nervous excitement in the pit of my stomach. Again the questions came: Will this really work? Will we truly bond? Will I have to go back to the cane?

"Clark!" "Clark Roberts!" I was jarred by the sound of my name. I grabbed the leash tightly. I heard my instructor say, "Relax, Clark; remember what you've been taught." I was then given the go-ahead; I reached out with sweaty palms and nervously took hold of the harness, adrenalin coursing through my body. I gave the command to proceed forward and my guide dog began walking with me, leading me, guiding me down the sidewalk. Although we only walked a short distance, I felt like I had just completed a marathon and won! This was the beginning of freedom and of a new-found confidence. This was also the beginning of friendships, relationships, and bonds forged out of sight loss. This was a tool that gave me a new kind of trust and connection—I could feel the weight of my sight loss lift from me. I was free! I set the cane in the corner of my closet to collect dust.

CHAPTER FOUR

Freedom of Mobility – Missy

A TIME TO TRUST

It was 1986. I was 32 and had arrived at Guide Dogs for the Blind—ready for a change and excited. As I spent those first twenty-eight days getting to know Missy, I didn't know what to expect.

Burke Bordner, Missy, and Clark

At this time in my journey with blindness, to me, this was like getting my first car. Freedom, freedom of mobility! I was excited and yet nervous. I did not know what kind of dog I would be getting and, like my first car, I didn't know the make or the model. You never know if you are getting a laid-back Retriever, (middle-of-the-road dog) or a high-strung "Mr.-work-all-day-long" dog. I didn't know what would happen the first time I took hold of the harness handle and gave the command "forward." Directing your dog for the first time is like sitting in a vehicle with the engine idling, steering wheel in hand, not knowing what to expect until you step on the accelerator and pop the clutch. And then you realize, wait! I can't drive! I can't steer! hold on—I can't see! I don't know which direction this car (dog) will take me! How do I stop! Where will I stop and how am I going to get back to where I started? Now was the time to time to trust.

As I was being introduced to Missy, a beautiful Golden Retriever, the representative from Guide Dogs explained the different breeds of working dogs this way:

German Shepherds are the happiest if they can work hard and long - we'll call them the Dodge Durango with a Hemi!

Labradors are reliable and will adapt to whatever lifestyle and pace is required - we'll call them the Subaru Outback of guide dogs.

Last, but certainly not least, is the Golden Retriever. Now a Golden is a very happy-go-lucky, laid-back dog, content to say, "If I work today, that is fine; but if I can put it off until tomorrow, that is even better!" Without a doubt, this would be the Volkswagen bus of the guide dog family.

Missy, or as I sometimes would call her, "Little Miss Mischief," was definitely a dog that allowed me to go for a nice walk at a well-adjusted pace and would do her job to the letter. But don't let that fool you, she was also very content to lie around the house and just be Missy.

POP, DROP AND ROLL

Missy had been raised by Burke Bordner, an eleven-year-old student, and his family in Redmond, Washington. Being a family of five, there was never a shortage of popcorn. Now we are not talking about microwave popcorn, but rather the real deal: oil, a hot pan, quick wrist, and the aroma of melting butter. POP, SNAP—all you need now is the bowl.

When Missy caught wind with her ever-active nose of popcorn being popped, it would send her into what is called, the "golden wiggle." Her front half would go one direction, and her back half would go the opposite, with the tail and the legs also wagging and jumping. All you had to do was rattle the pan and there she was waiting for you to drop a couple of kernels. You could see the hope in her eyes, hope that you would stumble and drop the entire bowl and it would come rolling over to her. She was always ready to lend a helping tongue so that you did not need to exert your energy cleaning up the spill.

HERSHEY'S KISSES

Like most Retrievers, Missy had an infatuation with food (any type of food). One day I was going to a meeting with Betty, Burke's aunt. Now, whenever Betty and I would go anywhere we would always be deep in conversation. This particular day Betty had a bag of Hershey's Kisses in her purse, which was sitting behind her seat in the van. The bag, although open, had hardly been eaten. Missy, who always sat in the backseat, soon discovered the bag. When we arrived at our destination we found that the bag of Kisses was almost completely gone and next to her purse was a pile of foil wrappers.

While Betty and I had been focused on our conversation we thought that Missy was sleeping quietly in the back seat. To our surprise instead, she had been gently unwrapping each chocolate kiss leaving only the wrapper behind, to this day we are not quite certain how she did it, but you can be sure that no one ever left chocolate out again.

RETIRING MISSY

After guiding for about six years, Missy began showing signs of losing her focus. There were moments when she would hesitate and balk as we moved forward. At one point she almost walked me in front of a car. I began to stop going out unless absolutely necessary. I always thought that if I could have sat down and had a conversation with her she would have said, "Clark, I'm tired and I want to stop working." The bond that a person has with their guide dog is strong. You are a team and, as a team, there is a deep connection in the way you work together. My teammate was no longer in the game.

I notified Guide Dogs for the Blind about my concerns and they sent out a Field Representative to evaluate Missy. She passed with flying colors. It was like having something wrong with your car, you heard the squeaky brakes, you felt the jerking of the car when you would apply the brakes, but as soon as you took it to the service station—no squeak, no jerking, no problem. The representative and I spent time discussing my options. He wanted to be sure I really wanted to retire Missy—after all, to him she seemed fine. But for me, the trust was gone. That total sold-out confidence in my ability to go out of the house and proceed safely from point A to point B was gone. I had doubts and I could not afford to have doubts—there was too much riding on this.

The decision was made and Missy retired. We called the Bordner family and asked if they would like Missy back. Their lifestyle at that time was not conducive to having a retired guide dog in their home. After the puppy raising family says no to taking the guide dog back, the responsibility falls back to the guide dog user. I spoke with my family and it was decided that Missy would go and live with our close family friends, the McCartneys. I felt good about the decision and knew that Missy was in a safe place, feeling loved and cared for. Missy had given me freedom of mobility and Guide Dogs had given me Missy—I was ready and excited to go through the process again.

CHAPTER FIVE

Led by a Shepherd – Toddy

UNDERCOVER DRUG DOG

In December of 1994 I was back in California at the San Rafael Guide Dogs for the Blind campus. I had just graduated with Toddy, an 85-lb. German Shepherd with saddleback coloring and bright brown eyes. My cousin Sharon, who was living in the Bay area, arranged for me to speak in two different high schools, both located in the inner city of Oakland. I arrived that morning to be informed that they were going to have me give three different presentations. Not a problem, I thought. It would be a good day of getting to know the students and helping them to understand what it was like to live life without physical sight. Shortly after ending the first presentation, the presiding teacher decided that we needed to move to a different room in the school. "Okay," I thought, "no problem, we will just casually walk with her through the building to the other area." I grabbed Toddy's harness and off we went through the halls of the high school.

It soon became apparent that we were causing some type of commotion and uneasiness as we navigated the hallways. Toddy was a big German Shepherd and, to many people, that meant a police dog. As we passed by, I could hear kids whispering while they were opening and closing their lockers, shoes shuffling on the old tile floor. All of a sudden, from down the hall came a yell—not a whisper, not quiet talking, just a loud yell: "Stash the drugs, here comes the drug dog!" My cousin and the teacher turned to me and without missing a beat stated, "Perhaps we should have you come down about once a month just to walk the halls!" Smiling to myself, I headed to the next classroom.

AIRPORT SECURITY

Often, during Toddy's working life, he and I would find ourselves in an airport. My motivational business would have us traveling from city to city speaking to schools and businesses. There were many occasions when people would stop us to ask directions, flight departure times or where their gate was.

Many of these times I would be accompanied by Rick Baker. Rick had a great sense of humor and a mischievous way about him. I would show up wearing my police-blue Guide Dog jacket with reflection stripes down the arms and the Guide Dog logo on the left front of the jacket. Rick would forget to take off his company ID badge and it would be attached to the collar on his jacket. These distinguishing "uniform" looks, and the fact that I was walking with a German Shepherd, made us look like airport employees. Rick, being the comedian that he was—and loving a good joke myself—would play along, directing people to their flights, answering questions about the airport, and sending people to the restrooms.

This was only the beginning of some of the mischief Toddy, Rick and I would get into!

DOUBLE-TALL HOT TODDY

One afternoon Rick and I had some time to kill before going to our next appointment so we walked into the Juanita Starbucks. Now mind you, this was in the mid-1990s when Starbucks was still a little coffee house just beginning to gain in popularity. Walking up to the counter, we ordered our coffee and then sat down to enjoy some conversation. Before we could even take our first sip, an employee came up to me and got within inches of my face stating, "Sir, you and your dog need to leave right now." Rick quickly jumped up and stated, "It's not just a dog," then went to the restroom leaving me sitting there to defend myself. Again the employee stated, "Sir, you need to take your coffee and you and your dog need to leave NOW." I stood up, calmed myself and went into education mode. I quickly realized that education was not going to work, for you cannot educate an ignorant person who refuses to learn. As I faced him, realizing that he was inches away from me, I was expecting him to grab my shirt and physically remove me from the premises. Rick chose that time to come back to the table and we decided to leave on our own. Exiting the store, we could see the manager discussing with the employee what had just happened.

I never did find out the outcome at that particular store, but we did take the time to contact Starbuck's corporate office to help educate them on how to interact with a blind person and a working guide dog. Let's just say that both Rick and I enjoyed free coffee for a while after that! Something about that encounter must have worked. Over the years, I have been very impressed with the courtesy and the respect that Starbucks employees have shown me and my various guide dogs. I would like to think that in some small way we helped to make that happen.

CAR WASH

Two of my ski buddies decided between Christmas and New Year's that it would be great to take a road trip from Seattle to Canada and ski Big White. On this particular trip, Toddy would stay home and enjoy being a "normal" dog for a few days with Rick. Rick was familiar with the rules regarding proper guide dog etiquette (although familiar with the rules, he also enjoyed breaking them). This meant that Rick knew that if he was going to go into any facility with Toddy, Toddy had to be dressed in his harness.

One day Rick decided to take his daughter's red Toyota Celica to the car wash; this particular December day was cool, but clear and sunny. It was the kind of day that makes you glad to live in the beautiful Northwest. Rick put on his overcoat and sunglasses and dressed Toddy in his harness. Once ready, off they went to the car wash with Rick driving and Toddy riding expectantly in the front seat.

Upon reaching the car wash, a person generally takes a number, puts their car in line on the conveyor belt and then gets out of the car and sits in the waiting room. Not Rick—he was feeling a little mischievous and grabbed Toddy's leash and harness, proceeding to work Toddy to the coffee stand to grab a cup and stay warm in the morning sunshine. Standing there with sunglasses on, coffee in hand, and this beautiful German Shepherd guide dog patiently waiting next to him, Rick was quite the picture of a visually-impaired person. A woman came up to him and asked if she could pet Toddy. Rick answered that Toddy was working, but "yes," she could pet him since she had asked so politely.

After a few minutes, Rick glanced at the reader board and saw his number flash—his car was done and ready for him. Rick grabbed hold of Toddy's harness handle and gave the command "forward." He then proceeded to work him to the driver's side door, opened it and allowed Toddy to hop in and settle into the passenger's seat. Rick got in, started the car and drove off—leaving a group of people staring at his tail lights, eyes wide, mouths hanging open, all wondering how on earth a blind guy could drive!

LED BY A SHEPHERD

Toddy and I had been invited to fly to Arizona to visit Rick, who had recently moved to Phoenix. When we flew in, we were greeted by a balmy February breeze, blue sky and the warm sunshine of the desert. I had to remind myself what month it was. I realized that there were people living in parts of the country where they still had snow up to their waist and icicles forming on the eaves.

Toddy settled in for the car ride, sitting in the back seat, head hanging out the window, tongue wagging in the wind enjoying the fresh air. Rick asked me what I would like to do. Since I was new to Phoenix, I said it was up to him and he suggested a place called Rawhide. Rawhide, Rick informed me, was a renovated old western town situated in two square miles of desert. This was a popular attraction for tourists, corporate events, and rodeos. I thought this sounded like a lot of fun so off we went. As we parked the car, Toddy and I breathed in the fresh scent of sagebrush, wild flowers and other aromas of the desert.

Approaching Main Street, we were greeted by the citizens of Rawhide—dressed in jeans, cowboy boots, and western hats, they greeted us with a great big "howdy." Rick and I went into the saloon and sauntered up to the long wooden bar. I took in the smell of aged tobacco, dust and the faint scent of leather. We found a couple of rustic bar stools and grabbed a nice cold bottle of water. After enjoying the water we exited back out into the warmth of the day and walked along on the wooden boardwalk. We paused to watch two gunfighters facing off in a simulated gunfight on Main Street in the Wild West. These men were dressed in denim jeans, boots and spurs, cowboy hats and leather holsters with six shooters sitting on their hip. As they stared at each other and shouted slander back and forth, you could feel the tension in the air, hear the crackle of gunfire, and a moan as a gunfighter fell to the ground. I stood there smiling as I took in everything that was happening around me and soaked up the amazing heat from the Phoenix sun.

After watching this, we decided to take a stroll and look at the rest of the town. This took us past the jail, empty except for the dust from the past. We then proceeded to the blacksmith shop where the blacksmith was working in the sun with a horseshoe, pounding it on an anvil as he had just fired it over an open flame. Departing from the blacksmith shop we continued to wander and talk and enjoy the sunshine. As we strolled down the dusty street, we came upon a patch of grass where a small band of sheep were chewing their cud, sunning, and enjoying the warmth of the day. Passing them, we soon realized we were at the end of the street and turned around to meander our way back to where we'd started from. As we walked we paid little attention to what was behind us. We continued back down the street past the blacksmith shop, past the jail, and past the center of town. It was about this time that Rick looked over his shoulder and said, "Don't look now, but you have eight sheep following you in single file." People stood to the side, watching us as if we were part of the events of the day. I smile and laugh every time I remember the day that the sheep in Rawhide were led by a German Shepherd!

DISNEY DOG

In 1996, I attended a conference in Anaheim, California. When the conference ended, I needed to find a way to return to the airport. Because Anaheim is next door to Disneyland, they have airport buses that make a circuit to all of the hotels close to Disneyland and then take you to your designated airline. You would see people getting on and off the buses wearing mouse ears, carrying stuffed animals and holding tightly to balloons. Since Toddy and I were the first to be picked up at our hotel, we boarded and sat in the very front seat as you enter the bus. The only thing separating us from the stairs and the passengers boarding was a small metal partition between our seat and the steps. The partition was chest high for me, but as you walked up the steps it was right at eye level for passengers.

Toddy was sitting down with his head and nose above the partition and was being a very obedient guide dog. He was not moving, not blinking an eye and, in fact, looked lifeless. The bus pulled up to our next stop and the door opened. A woman started to get on the bus, all the while glancing over at this large, very still Shepherd. Keeping a close eye on Toddy, she stepped up the stairs and again just stared. All of a sudden Toddy wiggled his ears and touched her arm with his nose! Well, let me tell you, this lady back-peddled so

31

fast off of that bus she nearly fell out. I am sure she will never forget how life-like those Disney stuffed animals could be!!

GOING UP, GOING DOWN?

Traveling with Toddy was always an adventure and our trip to Orlando was no different. We were attending a conference in Orlando and were staying in a large hotel on the 18th floor. The conference room that we were using was located in a daylight basement built into the hill.

This particular afternoon I needed to go back to my room to feed Toddy and then take him outside so that he could do his business. I jumped on the elevator, quickly went to the room, fed him, and took him out to do his business, all as planned—or so I thought. When Toddy was finished outside I needed to return to my room to quickly grab something—so we jumped on the elevator, went to the room and then returned to the elevator. Before I got the button pushed to head downward, the elevator went up two floors to grab three more gentlemen. As they stepped in, there was much conversation about how good-looking Toddy was and I could feel him lean into a hand for a quick ear scratching. As the elevator headed down, we stopped once more and picked up a couple with their baby in a stroller.

Our next stop was the lobby, where everyone except Toddy and I exited because we were headed to the convention floor, one more level down. Everyone said goodbye to me and to Toddy and asked if I needed any assistance with the buttons. I said, "No, thank you," and the door closed; I found the panel and pushed the button—nothing. I pushed it again and, again, nothing happened. I thought that perhaps someone had helpfully selected the button for me and had overridden my command. So again, I pushed the button—nothing! I then tried pushing the button for my floor to see if the elevator would go up and, again, no movement whatsoever! I realized that the elevator was not going anywhere and Toddy and I were trapped. My fingers quickly examined the huge bank of buttons and every button was marked in Braille, every button that is except for two (which I discovered later were the emergency button and the button to indicate where the internal phone was located in the case of an emergency). This was Murphy's Law at its best.

After a few short minutes and a few short prayers, I remembered that the elevator was sitting at the lobby level. I reasoned that there must be people coming and going by the elevator door. Now, I am a man who is not afraid to make noise so I started yelling and pounding on the door. I could feel Toddy looking up at me as if to say, "What on earth are you doing? Calm down and quit freaking out." It felt like time had stopped and I felt myself begin to really panic when, in reality, it was only a matter of minutes before my yelling and pounding grabbed the attention of those in the lobby. As they came to my rescue, one person asked how many people were in the elevator with me. I let them know it was just me and a dog. After a pause on the other side of the door, a few questions like *"What's a dog doing in the elevator?"*—then silence. After a few more minutes, the door sprang open. Toddy jumped out of the elevator so quickly that it felt like he had come right out of his harness. The sight of this 85-pound, brown and black German Shepherd lunging out of the elevator made a pretty clear statement to all that we were both happy to be released.

*Maria Wolfe receives "first touch"
as Toddy's puppy raiser*

*Toddy gets dressed in his "Guide Dog
Puppy in Training" jacket*

Toddy relaxes after play time

*Maria and Toddy with litter mates,
Travler and Tisha*

Don't worry, Toddy, you'll grow into it!

Maria and Toddy spending quality time before Toddy goes to Guide Dogs to meet me.

CHAPTER SIX

My Corporate Lady – Lacey

Clark and Lacey -- 1998

ADVENTURES OF LACEY

In 1998 I had the pleasure of meeting my fourth guide dog, Lacey. Lacey was a black Labrador who was raised for the first year of her life by a gentleman named Rand Morimoto in the San Francisco Bay area. Rand worked as a computer consultant and frequently traveled across the country on business. Because of this, when I received Lacey as my guide dog she came equipped with over 150,000 air miles; imagine my disappointment when I found out the air miles were not transferable! Lacey was a sleek black Lab with smoky dark eyes and a wonderful personality. I knew right away that God had worked this plan perfectly. I was traveling around the country more frequently as I shared my story in schools, businesses, and churches, and it only made sense to be teamed up with a guide dog that could move through an airport like a hot knife through butter. I never felt more confident navigating my way through a busy airport than I did with Lacey in harness.

LACEY'S FIRST FLIGHT

Lacey's ability to work an airport came after much training and traveling with Rand. Shortly after Rand received Lacey, training and travel began for this guide puppy. Rand had a business meeting that made it necessary for him to fly from San Francisco to Denver, he decided that since he had signed up to socialize Lacey and help train her for Guide Dogs for the Blind, he would take her along on their first of many business trips. Because she was barely potty-trained, Rick decided that he would not fly straight through to Denver but stop in Salt Lake to give Lacey the opportunity to do her business during a layover.

Imagine the attention that this coal black puppy received as she boarded the plane. Lacey, in her petite green jacket that read "Guide Dog Puppy in Training" walked beside Rand, her small feet finding a path amongst all the passengers as they boarded first class. The flight attendants and passengers wanted desperately to reach out to pet this precious little puppy, but seeing her jacket and realizing that she was "on the job," restrained themselves from doing so.
Upon reaching their seat, Rand settled Lacey comfortably on the floor just under his feet. She curled into a little ball and promptly fell asleep. As the plane began its steep climb, Rand glanced down to check on Lacey; to his surprise, she was no

Lacey's first flight Recreated compliments of Hudson Portrait Studios and the Seattle Museum of Flight

longer under his seat. Looking around, he did not see her anywhere. Almost at this exact time he heard a woman's voice several rows behind him cry out, "I have a puppy!"

During the very steep ascent, Lacey had slid under the seats only to find herself seven rows back sitting at the feet of a complete stranger. It took the rest of the short flight to Salt Lake for Rand to get Lacey back as the passengers each took turns cuddling her.

Once on the ground, Rand took Lacey out to do her business. When he and Lacey returned to their seat, Rand realized that keeping Lacey on the floor was not going to work. Knowing that he had to have her securely stowed he had a dilemma on his hands. Surveying the area, Rand spotted the magazine pouch on the back of the seat in front of him. He reached forward, pulled the pouch back, emptied it of its contents, and placed Lacey inside. Looking up at him with trusting eyes, Lacey snuggled in for the duration of the flight.

BILL GATES' HOME

As stated previously, Rand traveled quite extensively and had the opportunity to meet many people and see many sights and places. During the time that he was raising Lacey, she went everywhere with him. This even included sharing the invitation with her, when he had been invited to a meeting with Bill Gates at the Gates family estate on the shores of beautiful Lake Washington. During the course of the evening, Lacey needed to potty so Rand took her outside to do her business. While Rand was waiting for Lacey to finish up, Bill came out and asked him, "What is your dog doing on my new lawn?" Rand quickly replied back, "Better your lawn, than your carpet!" That night Lacey left more than just a good impression!

PRESIDENTIAL ENCOUNTER

Many times Rand would find himself running late for appointments and meetings. This particular day was one of those times. As he approached the hotel where he was supposed to have a business meeting he found the streets were blocked off. This was not a problem since he knew his way in and out of town and took a short cut to his destination. He parked the car, grabbed Lacey and his bag and, to avoid being late, decided to use the service elevator. He entered and was about to push the button to travel up to his floor when the elevator reopened and he was met by two security guards and President and Mrs. Clinton. They exchanged pleasantries and, after the security guards checked Rand's ID, he and Lacey traveled the rest of the way in the elevator with President Clinton telling Rand all about Buddy, their chocolate Lab and the country's First Dog.

MEETING THE BIG DOGS

As Rand traveled, he took Lacey with him to as many meetings and events across the country as he could to continue to prepare her for her life after

37

puppy training. These social events help the dog to learn how to...well not act like a dog in public. As Rand soon learned, he could train Lacey to lie quietly under a boardroom table and be as invisible as possible. The challenge was not Lacey, but rather training the meeting attendees and corporate businessmen and women to ignore the cute little puppy. Many times, prior to meetings, the attendees—despite being in their business suits—would be on the floor playing with Lacey. During meetings, it was not unusual to see one or two of them slipping Lacey an ice cube under the conference room table and reaching down to get one more "scritch."

A BOY AND HIS DOG!

Baseball buddies - 2000

Jacob and Lacey paddle boating - 1999

Jacob and Lacey - 2008

During that year of 1998, my life changed drastically. Not only was I getting a new guide dog, but I had a fiancé, Karrie, and her eight-year-old son, Jacob, waiting in anticipation to see what kind of a dog I would be getting. When I received Lacey, I immediately called them to let them know that there would be a loving black Lab coming home with me. It was then that I learned that there is nothing like the bond that a dog can bring to a new family, especially when it's about a boy and his dog! Lacey helped us to transition into our new life together.

In past years, I would never have allowed my guide dog to sleep on a bed, let alone a bed in another room. So when Jacob asked, I gave in and allowed Lacey to sleep at his feet each night. It was a new experience for me, having a guide dog with a family, too. She quickly adjusted to the rhythm of life with her new boy and he bonded quickly with her. It was fun and memorable to watch them run around the yard and house in a game of chase ending with a vigorous match of tug-o-war. There were times when I wondered if she remembered she was my guide dog first. I can almost guarantee you that Jacob claimed her as his dog first and my dog second.

LACEY'S PUPPIES

One evening in 2002, my wife Karrie and I were relaxing in our living room with Lacey on the floor. As we were sitting there, Becca, our two-year-old, came in the room, blonde curls cascading around her beautiful blue eyes. She climbed up on the couch and stared intensely at Miss Lacey. All of a sudden she jumped up and disappeared up the stairs. It wasn't long before she returned with her little arms tightly clutching a fuzzy mass of stuffed animals. Bears and bunnies were hanging on by their little stuffed legs, ears lopsided, with Beanie Baby giraffes and baby dolls ready to fall to the ground. Becca proceeded to completely cover Lacey with stuffed animals. Every now and then, Lacey would lift her sleepy head and look up at Becca as if to say, "This is fun, what else can we do?" Never once did she give the impression that she was not enjoying this little girl in play. After Becca had placed the entire armful on Lacey, she disappeared upstairs and came back with more stuffed animals.

When she had finished piling all of her animals and baby dolls on top of Lacey, she stepped back to admire her work and smiled. It was then that we asked what she was doing. She turned and looked at us, as if to say, "You don't know?" With a bright smile and a toss of her golden ringlets, she said, "These are Lacey's puppies." We realized that this was the beginning of many years of "girl time" with Lacey and Becca.

Exhausted at the end of the day

Becca and Lacey spending "Girl Time"

RETIRING LACEY

Over the ten years that Lacey was my guide dog, she made quite an impact on our entire family. There was a heart connection that had taken place with all of us from the moment I received her. It's difficult to explain how deeply the bond is until the time comes to let go. This was not a white cane—the cane is a cold inanimate object; this dog, this guide dog, was willing to show unconditional love; she was smart and completely intent on pleasing everyone that she came into contact with. Lacey had the purest of hearts all of the time.

The average working life of a guide dog is seven years; those years came and went with Lacey and she was still working strong. When you have a working guide dog you always know in the back of your head that someday, somewhere, and in some situation, there will be that moment when the dog turns and looks at you and says, "I'm done, I'm tired, I want a change of pace." As strange as it may seem, even though you know that this moment— this epiphany—is coming, you are never prepared for it. When it does happen, you cannot imagine the feelings and the thoughts that go through your head as you realize that a significant change is about to happen to both of you. A working guide dog has been trained to be your eyes; to keep you safely out of harm's way; to get you from point A to point B. When these things change, and the safety of the guide dog user is in question as well as the safety and health of the guide dog, it is time to look at what should happen next.

40

Becca and Lacey - 2008

Clark and Lacey speaking in San Antonio - 1999

Our moment, (our epiphany) came when we booked an all-family trip to Disney World in the early spring of 2008. As I worked Lacey through the airport I noticed that her stamina and her precise navigation of the airport were no longer there. Instead of being focused on where we were walking, she was confused, nervous, and unsure of her steps. As we maneuvered through the serpentine, Lacey would try to cut under the divider instead of staying in her lane. She hesitated when stepping onto the escalator and would stop for no apparent reason. When we got to Florida, the heat, the humidity, and the pace was too much for Lacey. Karrie and the rest of our family noticed that she just seemed tired. She would look at me and the rest of us as if to say, "Do I really have to continue—can't I just sit by the pool and enjoy my vacation?" She was done, she was ready, and she was exhausted.

Ten years is a long time and our entire family was as invested in Lacey's well-being as I was. Years earlier, Karrie's brother-in-law Jerry had told his daughter Janaye (who from day one had wanted Lacey to live with them) that "No," their family would not be getting Lacey at any time. Something on this trip changed that decision and he came up to me and said, "Clark, when you and Lacey are ready, we would love to take her." A greater gift could not have been given to me that day.

You might ask yourself why we did not just keep Lacey. As the guide dog user, I have first right of refusal to keep the retired guide. I chose not to do this for many reasons. It can be difficult for a retired guide dog to watch you as you leave the house with your new dog. As tired as they are, they still want to work, to be with you and please you. There can be jealousy that takes place between the two dogs and a feeling of loss for the retired guide. I felt Lacey deserved to have the love and attention that a new home could give her, a home that did not have a new working dog. This plan allowed us to have the best of all scenarios. Lacey was going to be with our family; she would be well loved and we knew that we could continue to see her as much as we wanted. So, as any new retiree would have it, Lacey took her trip to Florida, soaked up some sun, and officially retired six months later with family, familiarity and love.

Lacey's retirement trip, meeting Goofy at Disney World

Lacey, eight weeks. old —
Guide Puppy in Training

Clark and Lacey enjoying the lake

Lacey, a very well-trained Guide Dog!

Janaye with Lacey and Rocky

Lacey preparing for her role as flower dog at our wedding in 1999

Lacey racing across the yard

CHAPTER SEVEN

Arbuckle Samson Roberts

Clark and Arby 2009
Photo by Hudson Portrait Studios

WHAT'S IN A NAME?

On September 6, 2008, I woke up to cool Northwest weather in Seattle, Washington. Filled with anticipation, I knew that the overcast day would not dampen my spirits. You see, on this particular morning there was a flood of excitement as well as curiosity flowing through my veins. Today was the day that I would board a plane for my fifth trip since losing my eyesight to fly out to the campus of Guide Dogs for the Blind. On this trip I would be receiving my fifth guide dog; but, unlike previous trips, I would be heading to the Boring Oregon campus instead of San Rafael California. Boarding the airplane I was filled with excitement, I knew what was waiting for me in Oregon and I couldn't wait to meet my new guide dog. When I say I "knew," I only knew that I would be receiving a dog. Each time you receive a new dog it's a different experience and that is part of the wonder and excitement of it all. Arriving at the school, I would go to my room, unpack and get ready for the next day. I was hours away from learning who my new four-pawed friend would be.

I awoke the next morning to a knock at my door. Opening it, I was greeted by a representative from Guide Dogs who was there to escort me to the lounge where I would wait my turn to meet my new dog. Upon reaching the lounge, I was handed a new leash and was told that I would find a new harness in my room. As I waited, I took the cold stiff leather leash and began working it gently up and down in my hand. This would not only help to soften the new leather but also put my scent on it for my dog to recognize. My name was soon called and I walked outside into a beautiful fall day, typical of the Northwest—cool with a slight bite to the air. I felt the sun warming my face and smiled as I completed the walk to the trainer's room.

As I entered, I could hear the jangle of a collar and the anticipation of a tail thumping up against a desk (later, we would affectionately refer to this as the "tail of doom"). I was then told I would be receiving a male yellow Labrador named Arbuckle, or "Arby" for short. As I ran my hands over Arby, "seeing" him for the first time, I got to know his size, his coat, and the feel of his head and chest. In the background of this moment, Todd, the Trainer from Guide Dogs, was giving me a verbal description. He described a handsome male Labrador with a white belly, yellow body, and brindle coloring around his ears. He continued giving me the verbal tour by telling me Arby had large brown eyes that seemed to cut right into your heart, wrapping you in a warm hug. He said that Arby talked with his eyes, lifting his eyebrows up and down to emphasize how much he loves you and wants to please you. All of that description was seen in the moment that I met Arby. Close your eyes and imagine the scene. Me, sitting in a chair with Arby standing in front of me, wiggling with joy from head to tail, licking my face and pressing into me—a picture of pure joy.

Todd had told me that his name was Arbuckle. His name started with an A because he was from an "A" litter. This meant that all of his littermates also had names that started with A. I was then told that there were many possibilities for the origin of the name Arbuckle: there was a cartoon character named Fanny Arbuckle, there was a town in California called Arbuckle, and a brand of coffee made in Tucson, Arizona called Arbuckle's coffee. But none of these were the reason for his name. It really was quite simple; the people who had his mother for the breeding colony also happened to have the last name of Arbuckle and when this bundle of yellow joy was born in an "A" litter, they decided he looked like an Arbuckle. I am not sure what that means, considering that I have never physically seen Arby, but if it means that he is hard-working, funny, cuddly, quirky, crazy, loving, wiggly, and downright entertaining, then "yes," he is most definitely an Arbuckle.

MEETING THE FAMILY

Arby and I arrived back in Seattle in September of 2008. Up until the time we landed and walked out to the pickup area at the airport, none of my family had met or even seen a picture of Mr. Arbuckle. My daughter Becca was a little apprehensive about meeting Lacey's replacement. She was absolutely positive that she could not find a place in her heart for another dog. When the van pulled alongside the curb and the slider door opened, Arby launched himself into the backseat and began wiggling and licking Becca. Within seconds Becca and Arby were a wiggly, giggly mass of blond dog and curly-haired girl. Out of the moving mass came a voice, interjected with more giggles, "I love you, Arby! Oh yes, I love you!" Arby had been raised to charm any child or adult in 5.5 seconds and he was making good on it. Becca and Karrie fell in love instantly with this gorgeous yellow Labrador, Mr. Arbuckle Samson Roberts.

Becca and Arby chillin' after school

Arby at Duvall's Muddy Paws event, 2012

Arby waits for Becca after school

BACKSEAT DRIVER

I had Arby lay down on the floorboards of the van. As we pulled away from the curb, Karrie and I both expected him to sit there behind the passenger's seat, next to the double-bench seat; after all, this is where Miss Lacey used to sit. She would get in the van, turn around a couple of times and lay down for the duration of the trip, very calm and very lady-like. Not so with Arby! As Karrie was driving and Becca was petting Arbuckle Samson (as my kids call him), he kept moving to the space between the driver's seat and the passenger's seat. He would then park himself right in front of Becca who was sitting in the second seat. Sitting in front of Becca, he would take his head and bump it up under Karrie's right elbow. He would bump his head and take his nose and work his way under her arm while she was driving until she relented and let him rest his head on her lap and sit beside her. We had Becca take his leash and put him back on the side but, again, Arby worked his way between the seats and would bump his head under Karrie's arm repeatedly. She looked at me and laughed, saying, "We may have trouble training him to sit on the side of the van." As we continued driving home, Karrie asked me to

contact Jan Clark and inquire as to how Arby used to ride in their car. Sure enough, Jan verified that indeed this was his place. While Arby was a puppy he would travel with his puppy-raising family in their Ford Expedition. Arby, being a dog who craves attention, decided that he should ride up front with the driver. He would then sit with his bottom on the second seat, back legs dangling off the seat, front legs on the ground and his head under the driver's elbow. Whether Karrie wanted it or not, she had a new backseat driver.

One of the many hats of Arby

STINKY CLOTHES

Most dogs like to roll and play in freshly mowed grass, stink weeds and piles of dead leaves—anything that is odiferous. But truly, there are some things that no one should have to smell—and certainly would not want their dog rolling in. One of those is the fresh, or not so fresh, smell of stinky, pungent, sweaty, been-sitting-in-the-dark-corner-of-a-bedroom-for-too-many-days workout clothes. Our son Jacob played football in high school and would practice daily. The entire team had an agreement that they would not wash their workout clothes until the weekend. Saturday came and out came his clothes, dirt so thick that they could stand up on their own. One of those afternoons as the pile of clothes sat on the floor waiting their turn for the wash, in came Arby. One would expect a normal dog to turn up his nose and run the opposite direction of these clothes; after all, that is what we all wanted to do. But not Arby—shoving his nose deep into the pile, he sniffed and sniffed as if to say, "Ahhh, Heaven." Arby proceeded to flop onto the pile, rolling around, legs flying in all directions, arching his back, twisting and turning—all the while making deep rumbling guttural noises of sheer joy.

Only a young male dog could possibly understand and appreciate the stench of a teenage boy. The clothes were not the only thing that got washed that day.

DOG PADDLE

My mother- and father-in-law have a house on Coeur d'Alene Lake in Idaho where we go for our summer vacations. The home is rustic in style, with a wraparound porch and large exposed rocks on the lower half. It is set up off of the water, across the road and tucked back into a beautifully wooded area.

Arby drying off after his swim

To get to the lake you have to walk down a narrow, steep trail. Then you have to walk across a path that is equally as steep and narrow with loose gravel and no shoulder. This can prove to be quite challenging for a person with sight, let alone one who is blind. But the only way to the lake was down the trail. Once there, we had no desire to go back up, so we would pack accordingly and plan to spend hours just soaking in the sun.

The first summer that I had Arby was hot, with days well into the 90s. Those temperatures made it easy to head down to the dock to enjoy the water and the sun. One day the temperature continued to rise—after a while it was becoming very

Arby insists on drinking at the lake

obvious that not only were we feeling the heat, but Arby was getting a little toasty, as well. Now, as you might know, the Labrador as a breed is known for its ability to swim and retrieve in the water—or so we thought. We all tried to coax him into the water but he was having none of it. Jacob knew that if he got Arby excited he would do anything. Before we knew it, Jacob came running down the length of the dock, calling out to Arby. You could feel the wooden slates shaking with each of his steps as he raced toward the edge with

Arby hot on his heels. Jacob jumped in and Arby followed, although it quickly became apparent that Arby had surprised himself by jumping in! Jacob had jumped in on the lake side of the dock so Arby decided to follow Jacob doing the best doggy paddle he could to get to shore. As Arby began swimming, there was a look in his eyes that said, "Water, I love to drink water!" It was that unfortunate realization that got him into trouble.

As we watched, Arby with his mouth wide open, was lapping up water with his tongue and clearly choking as he swam. This goofy dog was making no progress towards shore and was much more interested in drinking the lake than swimming. Eventually, Arby began taking on more water than he could swim through and Jacob had to swim out to rescue the waterlogged dog.

WORKING THE SYSTEM

In 2010, our family traveled to Hawaii for a much-needed vacation. As we finalized our plans, it was decided that we would leave Arby at home because of the strict animal regulations when bringing an animal onto the islands. After placing several calls to different friends and family, my wife's cousin and her family won the right to dog-sit for eight wonderful days. Now to be honest with you, I was feeling pretty good about the arrangements for Arby's care. I mean, after all, I could not go wrong with an attorney, a police officer and three teenagers watching over my dog. We took Arby up to Everett, dropped him off with his bed, his toys, his food, and a letter outlining the care and feeding of a guide dog. I told them this would be a piece of cake since Arby was very well- trained and was used to being on his tie-down during the day. I let them know that if they just took him out in the morning and again at night to potty and play a bit he would be very happy.

When we dropped Arby off on Sunday, the house was full of activity and the family was extremely excited to have Arby there. As previously stated, Arby loves people and loves to be the center of attention. So when Monday came, everyone left for school and for work and the house got quiet. This left Arby feeling a little dejected and lonely; after all, his family was gone and he was in an unfamiliar house with no one around. That night when the door opened and Ron (a policeman) came into the house, Arby sat up and stretched himself to the very end of his tie-down, looking at Ron as if to say, "Please, Oh Please!—let me off my tie-down!" Arby stared at Ron with his big brown eyes and worked his amazing eye brows; this all spoke volumes to Ron, who found himself caught in Arby's emotional entrapments. With Arby's body wiggling from head to tail, his entire body was on fire. It was all that Ron could do to get his tie-down undone—then bedlam broke loose. Arby took off running like a mad dog throughout the entire house, 0-60 in 5.5 seconds. Before Ron knew it, Arby launched himself like a jet-propelled missile, catching Ron off guard and, to his surprise, almost knocking him down. Even though Arby was an educated, well-trained guide dog, he was still a seventy-pound, three-year-old yellow Lab and a powerhouse who could get extremely excited. All he wanted to do from then on was wrestle with Ron until the teens came home and could take him outside to play with his rubber ring.

That night after everyone was in bed, Ron and Karen talked about what to do with Arby the next day. Ron's heart melted when he saw that big dog looking at him with those soulful eyes and he knew he could not leave him alone again. He thought to himself that if any of his peers on the police force stopped by, they might accuse him of entrapment of a K9. They decided that Karen would take Arby to work the next day. She would put this "junior partner" in his leather clothes and he would escort Karen to the law office.

The next morning, Arby sat up with excitement when Karen picked up his leash, not knowing where he was going but knowing that he was going somewhere. Upon reaching the law office, Karen told her coworkers this was her new "junior partner" and he was there to keep an eye on all of her clients from under the desk. Arby began looking forward to Karen grabbing her briefcase and keys and he would race to the door to wait for her. After jumping in the car, they would be off to the courthouse to deliver papers— Karen with her leather briefcase and Arby in his leather harness. Once in the car, Karen says Arby sat on the floor; but I envision he was sitting on the leather seats with the window halfway down, hanging his head out and saying, "This is the life!" Upon reaching the courthouse, Karen would grab his leash and in they would walk.

When we returned from Hawaii, we heard the story and were laughing at how Arby had pulled the wool over the eyes of both an attorney and a policeman. We knew he would have been okay just staying at their home during the day, but he had other ideas and redirected his case flawlessly. I honestly expected to find a legal document written and ready for signing letting me know that my working guide was now their property. Arby pleaded his case and was released from house arrest; his attorney Karen was more than happy to pardon him.

My bone, my best friend

*Picking out the perfect
Christmas tree*

Clark and Arby speaking for Young Life

We are "King of the Mountain!"

*Arby and his cousin Cody patiently
waiting to come in for dinner*

Is this the right pose?

Becca and Arby, snow day!

I wear my sunglasses at night...

Arby with Jacob at College graduation 2012

Family day at the corn maze

CHAPTER EIGHT

Connected by the Leash

Burke, Steve and Betty Bordner
Ron and Kay Kinssies
Bill Keogh
Mark and Jeannie Ferguson
Jack and Debra Hurley
Rick Baker
Rand Morimoto
Kelly and Jan Clark

The day that I first took hold of a guide dog harness, I could have never imagined how my life would change. Being connected to a guide dog allowed me to build relationships with the people that helped to raise and socialize my guide dogs. Not only those directly connected to my dogs, but also people that I have connected with because of my dogs. My journey has been an exciting one, and many of the people that I met along the way have continued to be part of it; friends, connected by the leash.

THE BORDNER FAMILY

I had my first guide dog, Missy, for a little over two years when I moved to Seattle, Washington. Not long after I moved, I received a newsletter from Guide Dogs for the Blind announcing that there was a puppy day at the Puyallup State Fair. I thought this would be a fun activity to attend and participate in as a guide dog user. I contacted one of the local puppy raisers and asked if she knew of anyone going to the fairgrounds that I could ride with. A few minutes later, I received a phone call from a woman named Betty Bordner. At that particular time, I did not know that Betty was the aunt of Burke who raised my first guide dog, Missy. You can imagine my surprise, when Betty picked me up and Burke was with her! My surprise was overshadowed by Missy's reaction. She began a full-body wiggle that started at the tip of her tail and rippled up and down her legs, crossing her shoulders and caused her entire body to shiver and shake, barely allowing me to hold her with the harness and leash.

During the ride to the fairgrounds, Burke was in the back seat with Missy who was overjoyed to see him and could not get enough attention. I sat in the front and visited with Betty. She and I quickly discovered that we had many things in common and talked nonstop about all of it. Betty was Burke's aunt and loved dogs; she was also present during much of Missy's time with Burke and had the opportunity to help socialize Missy. Betty and her husband Steve were very strong Christians and involved in their church, with choir, Bible study and youth group ministry. It only seemed natural that a few weeks later, Betty and I established a prayer ministry where we would call each other weekly and pray for puppy club members, family members and life events. To this day (twenty-four years later) we still call each other and pray for those in need. This would be the beginning of many visits to the Bordner house where Missy and I would hang out with the entire Bordner family and it became the foundation for a long-lasting friendship.

While spending time with the Bordner family, I had the opportunity to meet several other people belonging to the Redmond Puppy Club. This was the club that Burke had raised Missy in and I soon became an honorary member. On Friday evenings I would attend their meetings, answering questions about what it was like to be a guide dog user. I walked the group through demonstrations of a guide dog in use, and gave them tips on how to help the puppies become great guide dogs. I accompanied the club on "puppy outings" where the guide dog puppies are socialized in public. They do this by giving the puppies simple commands and opportunities to interact with real life situations. It was at one of these outings that I met the Kinssies family.

THE KINSSIES FAMILY

Ron and Kay Kinssies, their daughter Megan and their son Aaron, were helping to raise a puppy for Guide Dogs for the Blind. Aaron was in middle school and was the primary raiser as this was his 4-H project. When I met the family during an outing with the puppy club, we had an instant connection. Our friendship grew as we spent time together talking about guide dogs, puppies and the blessing of friendship. As I got to know them, I learned that they too were another very solid Christian family and our friendship deepened even more. It did not take long before I began spending weekends visiting their house and going to church with them at Overlake Christian Church in Redmond.

It is always amazing to me how God moves your life in directions that have undeniable impact on your future. The connections that we make at the time may not seem to make any sense, but later you can look back and it seems very clear. I love the saying, "Life is like a puzzle; what are you doing with the pieces?" I knew that God was very busy fitting pieces of my life together, forming an incredible masterpiece that I had yet to see. A very significant piece of my puzzle occurred in 1998 when, on a beautiful Sunday morning, Ron and Kay and I would drive to a little church called Coal Creek Chapel in Bellevue to visit. As Kay tells the story, they dropped me off and that was the last they ever saw of me. The reason—I walked into that little church and proceeded to meet my future wife. But that is another chapter for another book!

BILL KEOGH

While attending Overlake Christian Church ("Overlake") with Ron and Kay, they introduced me to their youth pastor, Bill Keogh. It didn't take long for the two of us to become fast friends. After all, we both loved dogs and had a passion for ministry; but the most important reason was that he could put up with my sense of humor and I with his!

One afternoon, Bill had some time to kill so I invited him to go tandem bike riding. He came straight from the church and changed into his riding clothes when he got to my apartment. It was at that time he discovered that he had forgotten his cycling shoes and socks. Undaunted by the idea of making a new fashion statement, Bill donned his leather-bottomed, buffed-up black dress shoes with his calf-high black dress socks and, with a grin (and a mischievous glint in his eyes), jumped on the front of the tandem. We were quite a sight—I in my bright orange and black "blind cyclist" jersey and Bill in his T-shirt, shorts, black dress socks and leather-bottomed shoes! Bill and I had many laughs over that ride. Laughs and memories that I was happy to share when I spoke to his junior high youth group at Overlake. This was the beginning of a great friendship with Bill and also the beginning of many speaking engagements with his youth group.

THE FERGUSON FAMILY

I would spend about four years with the Redmond Puppy Club and during that time was introduced to Alisha Ferguson and her parents, Mark and Jeannie. Alisha, a high school student, was raising Sheriff, a Golden Retriever guide puppy. As Alisha and I got to know each other, she discovered that I was just a normal guy with a crazy sense of humor who enjoyed hanging out and loved dogs.

It was with that in mind that she asked if I would be willing to attend the King County Fair in Enumclaw for a week with the puppy club. I was excited for the opportunity and during the week I was posed questions like, "What do you miss most about not having your vision?" and, "What is it like to experience the fairgrounds without the sense of sight?" It was interesting, I was ready for the questions, but I was never quite ready for the emotions that those questions evoked. I closed my eyes and really thought about my answers. What did I miss most about not having my vision? In the beginning, I did not want to discuss how my sight loss impacted me but I realized it was important to be open and answer people's questions. It was an important part of my journey, both for healing and for helping those around me to better understand me. I thought about my answers. I knew I missed looking into the sky and seeing the beauty of a rainbow after a rainstorm; watching as a horse runs carefree through a field, flipping its head and mane wildly as it enjoys the pure freedom of the run; sunrises and sunsets; pictures of family; a child's smile. So much of what I missed was a mystery until the moment the emotion hit me. As we were walking, the club members had an opportunity to observe how a blind person with their guide dog navigates in a high-foot-traffic setting such as a fair. I explained to them how I missed walking around on my own—moving in and out of the display barns, visiting the horse barns and looking into their gentle brown eyes, seeing the well-groomed, muscular livestock. I missed watching the flick of their tails and the grace with which they performed their jumps during dressage. The exhibit halls where the 4-H projects were displayed and Future Farmers of America had been a favorite of mine and now brought little joy. I could hear the laughter and discussion around me, but could not appreciate the visual results that were the center of the applause and discussions.

Yes, I did miss the visual element of the fair. But there were new memories for me to make and new elements to concentrate on. I loved the aroma of the food vendors, hotdogs, smoke from BBQs, popcorn, fresh-buttered corn-on-the-cob. I took in the sounds all around me—bubbling laughter from girls and boys as they enjoyed the roller coaster, the screams of terror and giggles and chants of "Do it again!" I allowed my mental videotapes to run as I took in the smell of leather; the scent of sweat from a calf-roping horse mixed with the resin of a bull rope. I could feel the excitement from a young rider getting ready to run the barrels; the aroma of cattle mixed with the earthy smell of hay and straw. I recognized the sweet smell of molasses on the dressed oats sitting in the feed buckets and could envision the horses eagerly waiting to eat; the conversations of people as they passed by, commenting on my guide dog, feeling them sweep a hand over the top of Missy's head. I did miss a lot visually, but I was being filled up with new memories and I cataloged each and every one.

It didn't matter if we were running errands, going to the fair, shopping or just hanging out. My friendship with Mark, Jeannie and Alisha continued to grow—a friendship connected by the leash.

THE HURLEY FAMILY

During the time that I participated with the Redmond Puppy Club, I met Jack and Deborah Hurley and their children Rose and Joseph, both of whom were in middle school and were raising a puppy for Guide Dogs for the Blind. Our friendship developed out of our love of dogs and the common theme that Guide Dogs continued to give us: one of selfless giving. We shared stories of guide dogs and the amazing adventures that the raisers took these puppies on as well as the journey that the puppies took them on. Jack and Deborah understood the magnitude and emotional impact of raising a puppy. They also saw firsthand through my life the importance of the guide dog and the Guide Dog program.

I accompanied the family to and from puppy club meetings as well as day trips to socialize the puppies at airports, malls, ferry rides and parks. During this time we would walk up and down escalators, ride elevators, dine in restaurants and walk through crowded areas. These activities helped the puppies to learn how to act appropriately as a guide in every day settings.

I still stay in touch with the Hurleys and have continued to be amazed by the friends God has put in my life—all because of a dog.

RICK BAKER

Over the years, no matter where I have been, finding a men's Bible study has always been a priority. One evening, during one of our Bible studies, I noticed that there was a new guy in our group. After chatting and catching up with some of the regulars there, he came over and introduced himself to me and to Toddy (my new guide dog, a beautiful German Shepherd I had received after retiring Missy). Actually, to be honest, he more or less introduced himself to the dog first and then to me! But nonetheless, his name was Rick Baker and, before I knew it, he had taken a liking to Toddy and to me and our friendship grew.

Rick was a corporate guy working for an aerospace company not far from where I lived. We hit it off and started hanging out together. Rick was outgoing, mischievous and sometimes quiet. It was during those incognito times, that you had to be on your guard. With him, you never quite knew what he was up to or what was going on upstairs in that mind of his. He enjoyed life—especially music and the outdoors. But even more than his hobbies, Rick loved Toddy. Upon Toddy's retirement, Rick didn't hesitate to ask if he could take him.

The protocol for retiring a guide dog was to first allow the guide dog user the option to keep the retired guide. Living in a small apartment and living on my own, it was not in Toddy's best interest to stay with me so that option was out. The second option was to give the dog back to the family that had raised him. Seeing that I was not going to keep him, Toddy was returned to his puppy-raising family in Sacramento. Toddy could not adjust to the slower pace and was not content to sit by and watch the other dogs go out and work. Tension grew among the dogs and Toddy again needed to come back and be relocated one more time. It was at that time I placed a phone call to a very enthusiastic Rick. When he picked up the phone I asked, "Rick, would you like to have Toddy come hang out with you for a permanent vacation?" He replied with an immediate, "Yes!"

From that moment onward, Toddy went to the sun-soaked landscape of Arizona to live out his retirement in a manner that any dog would be jealous of: relaxing by the pool, working on his tan, and being pampered by a man after his own heart.

RAND MORIMOTO

When I received my fourth guide dog, Lacey, in November of 1998, I had the honor of meeting Rand Morimoto. Rand worked as a computer consultant and his job required him to fly extensively across the U.S. Between the time that he had Lacey, from nine weeks old until she was a little over a year, Rand and Lacey would rack up over 150,000 air miles—unfortunately, nontransferable.

Rand shared stories with me about business meetings where men and women, dressed in their business attire, would get down on the floor to play with this little black Lab. I can imagine the scene: black and dark gray suits, crisp from the dry cleaner, immaculate creases, ties straight, and then down on the floor, suit pants wrinkled, ties askew, dark puppy hair clinging to white button-down shirts.

*Meeting Rand at the San Rafael
Guide Dog campus in 1998*

*Guinness - Rand's dog and
Guide Puppy Lacey*

*Lacey in her Guide Dog Puppy
In Training Jacket*

Rand not only raised Lacey, a dog that was a perfect fit for my life and my speaking business—he also helped me to develop and move that business to the next level. By donating a laptop to Ultimate Vision, Rand provided me with a tool necessary to travel and utilize technology on the go. Having the laptop with me allowed me to demonstrate to students the interactive screen reading program that I use. The hands-on demonstration helped the students better understand how a blind person stays connected in a technological world.

In 1999, Rand and his wife Kimber blessed my wife and I by attending our wedding—where they met our family and visited Lacey. Knowing that I was passionate about tandem bicycling, Rand then proceeded to donate air miles for me to fly to New York in September of 2002 to participate in the Face of America, a 9/11 Tribute Bicycling Event that started at Ground Zero and ended at the Pentagon.

Paying it forward is a term that Rand knows well and I am blessed because of his generous heart.

Clark, Rand, and Lacey after the graduation ceremony at Guide Dogs for the Blind in 1998

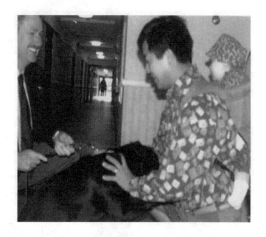

Rand and Lacey reunited at our wedding–1999

THE CLARK FAMILY

Lacey worked as my guide for almost ten years. After I retired her in 2008, I received my fifth and current guide dog Arby. At that time I was introduced to Jan and Kelly Clark, along with their five children, Kelsey, Caleb, Reuben, Nate, and Isabel. Raising Arby was a family event and, when Arby and I graduated from our training at Guide Dogs for the Blind, Jan, Kelsey and Isabel were there to represent their family and to celebrate Arby being placed with me as my guide.

Arbuckle ("Arby" for short) had been socialized by attending all of the kids' school and sporting events. Jan and Kelly took Arby to church each week and as a family they had prayed for the right person to be teamed with Arby. At the same time, my family was praying for my next guide dog to be one that could fit in with my life. I would need a dog that could work in business settings as well as schools and churches, and one that would be well adapted to hang out with both children and adults. You can imagine how excited I was when I received Arby and realized how well he met these criteria.

Jan, Kelly and I have stayed in touch from the day that I graduated with Arby from Guide Dogs. I have had the pleasure to go and speak a couple of times at Reuben, Nate and Isabel's school, Northwest Christian, in Spokane. The Clark family opened their home to me on both of those visits. While staying at their home, I was able to see firsthand how much each of them loved Arby and how he returned that love and sought out their attention.

While there, Jan told me how Arby used to lay at the top of the stairway with his head hanging down over the landing, keeping watch over the household. It was no surprise to any of us that, once he was back in their home, he took his place at the top of the stairs, keeping a watchful eye.

Arby and I now travel the country sharing our message of hope and encouragement through Diversity and

Clark and Arby with Kelsey, Jan, and Isabel, graduation 2008

Awareness Education. Educating people that living life with a disability does not mean that life stops. That life will have challenges, and it's how we choose to move through those challenges that counts. Teaching others to look at the skills and abilities within themselves and showing them how to use those challenges to live a life that is full.

I am blessed by a new friendship that I continue to build with the Clark family but, even more so, I have been blessed with my new guide dog, Arby. More than a dog, he is a friend and partner who has my trust and is truly a quirky character who loves life as much as I do.

The greatest blessing of all is to have a puppy raiser family love so much that they want to continue the relationship with me, with my guide dog, and with my own family. I hope you enjoy these pictures from the "Puppy Book" that the Clark family made for me.

Arby at 4 months

Looking back over all of these individuals, families and lifelong friends, I have come to realize that there is a common denominator. The leash connects me to my guide dogs, which connect me to the people that raised them, interacted with them and then chose to interact with me. The leash also connects me to those friendships that started because others reached out to my guide dogs, and then to me. But more than that, had I not had the faith to reach out and "grab hold of the leash," I would have never experienced the life and the relationships that I have now.

Shopping Buds

You can't see me

"Wait..."

Hoopfest was hot and crowded!
Arbuckle did great

Last day at the Clark home - 3/8/08

Arbuckle remembered us! - 9/20/08

Arby is always thirsty

Unforgettable

CHAPTER NINE
Short Dog Tails

DOG DAYS — THE EARLY YEARS *by Clark Roberts*

Growing Up with Barney

Growing up, we had a very special dog, Barney, who found his way into your heart very quickly. He was part Australian Shepherd and part Heinz 57, which is a mix of many breeds. Our family had acquired him through a local dog shelter in our community. Barney had many tricks up his sleeve and made it easy for anyone to love him.

Ice Cream Cones

The summers in Nampa, Idaho could get very hot, giving a whole new meaning to the term "The Dog Days of Summer." Barney enjoyed these days more than any other dog we knew. As each day came to an end, we all knew what was coming. Dairy Queen ice cream treats, cold, melting, sweet, and refreshing.

Gathering up the family, we would head to the car, opening the door for Barney to jump in. Without hesitation he would jump right into the front seat. That's right, no yelling shotgun, this seat was his! Hanging his head out of the front passenger's window, tongue wagging in the summer heat, Barney would anticipate his frozen treat. Whether it was vanilla, chocolate or a swirl of both, he would eat it the same way every time.

First, he would take his tongue and gently, in a very matter-of-fact manner, lick around the mountain of ice cream, being careful not to knock it off of its frozen throne. Next he would take the entire treat out of the cone, gulp the remaining ice cream down, and proceed to nibble the cone very slowly, savoring each and every bite. Barney never wasted a drop or left a single crumb on the seat of the car.

Love of Music

Not only did Barney have great taste in food, he was also a connoisseur of music. Good ole 'Barney had a little culture flowing through his doggie veins! My mom was a very accomplished pianist who had taught piano lessons and for years had played at church and for her family at home. It was not unusual for us to come home to mom practicing in preparation for Sunday services. But there were plenty of other times that she just played for sheer enjoyment.

Each time my mom sat down to play, Barney would come running into the room wagging his tail. He would race in and quickly take his place under the piano, lying down; he would then begin scooting as close as he could to my mom's feet (as if not to interfere with the pedals) and lay up against the soundboard. Barney would lie there listening and feeling every musical note that mom played. To this country dog with a little culture, this was Heaven, this was home.

Undercover Canine

Barney was essentially a housedog and, being a house dog, there was a set of rules that he was not allowed to break. One of those was that he was not allowed on the furniture, especially the beds. Somehow, though, Barney always found ways to sneak in a quick—dare I say it—CATNAP? When the family would leave the house, Barney would attack a bed, pulling down its covers before sleeping on the pillow. It was as if he waited, feigning sleep, eyes closed, sprawled out on the hardwood floor, waiting for the click of a closed door. Even if we were home we would never catch him in the act, he was that good! This undercover canine could make a quick escape, never getting caught in the actual act of his afternoon siesta. If you had just been in your room and you got up to leave for a moment, then quickly returned, you would find him sneaking out with his tail between his legs, the bed a mess and pillow warm.

Homewrecker Hound

During a family trip, Mom and Dad asked a young married couple, Annette and Jerry, to house sit for them. While house sitting, they would also be keeping an eye on Barney. One morning they woke up nice and early, made the bed and then went to the kitchen to have breakfast. Upon completion of breakfast, Annette went back to the master bedroom. She immediately came out and asked Jerry, "Why didn't you make the bed?" He assured his wife that he had made the bed, but she said, "Oh No You Didn't!" At that point, he walked back to the bedroom and sure enough, the bed was unmade. Puzzled, Jerry took a moment to make it, only to have Annette come back some time later to see the bed was again a mess.

As the week continued, Annette was getting frustrated with Jerry, Jerry was getting frustrated with the situation as well as feeling extremely confused, and Barney was enjoying little doggy naps at the expense of the young couple. One morning after Annette and Jerry had finished breakfast and were heading back to the bedroom, Annette caught Barney slinking out of the bedroom with head down and his tail between his legs. It was at that moment she realized that it had been Barney who had messed up the bed all the time. Jerry and Annette found much to laugh about as they realized the dog had pitted them against one another all week.

Locked in the Trunk

One summer our family was preparing to travel from Missoula, Montana to Alberta, Canada for a family reunion. We had two cars sitting in the driveway; our new car, a red Oldsmobile that we were going to drive to Canada, and our old car, a white Delta 88 Oldsmobile that we were trying to sell. Now the old car had an issue with the rear window, which had a leak around the seal that allowed water into the trunk. This made it necessary on warm days to open the trunk and let it dry out.

This particular afternoon while we were packing the car Barney decided to crawl into the back seat, as if to say "Okay everyone, I'm ready, let's go." But Barney was staying behind with our friend Colleen so we removed him from the car and he promptly jumped in the open trunk of the Delta 88 to sun himself.

We finished packing and closed the trunk on both vehicles. Waving goodbye to Colleen, we loaded all four kids in the backseat and, with Mom and Dad in the front, left for Canada. After driving for six hours we reached our destination and promptly received a call from Colleen. She asked, "Did you take Barney with you?" My dad answered, "No, isn't he there with you?" Colleen replied, "No, I can't find him anywhere."

Dad then instructed her to check under all of the beds and in the backyard; Barney was nowhere to be found. As we recounted the events of the day, we remembered what had happened when we were packing and told Colleen to check the trunk of the car. She tentatively began to open the trunk, expecting to find a dead dog, but instead was startled when a very exuberant Barney jumped up and began licking her face. He gave the impression of saying, "Why did it take you so long to come and find me in this stinky car? I am so happy to see you and now I will love you forever."

Cats and Dogs

Barney, like most dogs, had little tolerance for cats. He looked for them, he found them, and he chased them. He never caught or hurt them; he just liked a little excitement and a little spicing up of his life now and then. I am sure that all the neighborhood cats knew about Barney. Somewhere in the cat world, there was a poster showing a picture of a tri-colored Australian shepherd with a note by it to all cats that said, "Beware of this overzealous canine."

One evening as Dad took Barney out for his walk, he looked across the street and saw that the neighbor's living room light was on. Dad could see the family watching television with their cat resting in the windowsill. Barney also spotted the cat, putting himself into a full run as he raced toward their house. As quickly as he had taken off, he stopped, making a four-pawed stop right under the window and began sniffing the ground.

Before my dad had an opportunity to call him back and continue the walk, Barney stood up on his rear legs, put his front paws on the window ledge and placed his cold, wet nose on the glass. The cat continued to lie on the windowsill facing the living room, completely unaware of the danger lurking on the other side of the glass. At this exact moment, the cat turned and found himself face to face with Barney. This startled the cat so much that she did back flips and was scratching and clawing the curtains trying to get away. Flying fur and cat yawls could be seen and heard even from outside. The scene was chaotic as people from the house jumped up from the couch and the chairs. You could see them laughing and wondering what on earth was wrong with the cat. Outside Barney went undetected as he jumped down from the window and was once again off on his run through the neighborhood.

Beachcombing

One year, our family had the opportunity to travel from Southern Idaho where I grew up to Cannon Beach, Oregon to enjoy the sights and sounds of the ocean at a family friend's beach house. As we prepared to travel, we decided not to kennel Barney but rather take him for a fun family road trip and a visit to the beach.

The cabin was a beautiful, rustic beachcomber's delight located at the end of a long winding road. Surrounded by an old weathered cedar fence, it sat blanketed in the early morning mist. Stepping out of the car, we were greeted by a salty taste as the mist lingered on our skin. Thunderous sound filled our ears as it echoed up the hillside from the crashing waves below. Seagulls cried out to each other as they danced to the rhythm of nature.

To access the beach, we walked down a narrow wooden stairway that felt like it went on forever. Rounding the corner, the trees parted and you could see the ocean crashing on the beach. In the distance, sitting majestically in the middle of the view, was Haystack Rock. For the next few days, this would be our sanctuary.

The next morning, before most of us were up and ready for the day, my dad and Barney headed down to the beach. Barney bounded down the stairs and waited patiently at the bottom for my dad, who had his beachcombing bucket and shovel. Upon reaching the soft sand, Barney raced ahead feeling the freedom of the open beach. Once he reached the hard pan, he began barking, encouraging Dad to hurry up. (The hard pan is the area of wet sand left behind once the tide has gone out.) Barney was excited about his first trip to the beach and was ready to explore.

With Barney in front continuing to lead the way, he ran down the beach stopping every few feet to dig. Heavy, wet sand would fly from behind him; taking his nose he would put it under an object, flip it on the beach, give a little yip and be off and running again. When my dad reached the object that Barney had flipped up out of the sand, he would find that it was an untarnished whole sand dollar; happily he would add it to his collection in the bucket.

Each time my dad would slow to collect the treasure, Barney would race off again, yipping as if to say, "Come on, you're taking too long!" My dad would then put a little hustle in it and begin following Barney's trail of sand dollars like Hansel and Gretel and their trail of breadcrumbs. Each step brought him closer to Barney and soon his bucket overflowed. They continued this treasure hunt until they reached Haystack Rock.

Dad then called Barney and put him on his leash. Together they sat and enjoyed the quiet of the morning, the cool ocean breeze, seagulls calling out to the rising sun, and the waves crashing up and around the massive Haystack Rock. Just another day in a dog's life: dog's best friend, treasure hunting and beachcombing.

Breakfast Rolls

Growing up in our home was like living every day in a premier bed and breakfast, with Sunday morning being our favorite day of the week. Snuggling in comfortably for the last few moments of shuteye, your nose teased by the aroma of fresh-baked sweet rolls and coffee. Sunday mornings could get a little crazy with two brothers and a sister all trying to get ready for church, and breakfast became a comical session of each man (or woman) for himself.

My wonderful Canadian mother would be sure to vary the menu from week to week, but it always consisted of homemade sweet rolls of some variety— Orange rolls, caramel nut rolls or, on healthier mornings, bran muffins. No matter what the choice, it was always fresh and guaranteed to come with a hot cup of coffee and a glass of juice.

This particular morning the coffee had been brewed to the perfect strength; rolls were neatly arranged on a platter, still steaming with the heat from the oven. Pecans slowly trailed their way down the sides of warm caramel waterfalls. Unfortunately, this particular morning, for whatever reason, we were running late. Breakfast would have to wait.

As church concluded and we finished visiting with friends and family, it was time to head home. All of us knew what was waiting on the table. Once there, we were clamoring to see which one could get to the house the fastest. Racing out of the car, we were met by Barney. Nose down and tail between his tail, he gingerly slinked out moving in a peculiar manner with a side-to-side motion much like a duck waddling.

As I am writing this, I still chuckle when I think of the scene that day. As we reached the counter we saw that not only was the plate with the rolls missing, but also the butter. I remember the look on our faces when, after surveying the room, we discovered both plates on the floor, licked completely clean, sparkling like new. We stood amazed that the plates were not broken, and feeling a little angry and disheartened that we had been left out of the morning feast. Our disappointment and anger quickly turned to pity as our eyes were drawn to Barney. He had found a place to lie down in the corner, leaning on his side in a way that showed his swollen stomach. His eyes looked at us as if to say, "I can't believe I ate the whole thing!" Our hearts went out to this poor puppy, burping and feeling miserable, looking like he had just had his last supper.

THERE'S A DOG IN THERE? *by Janine Prindle*

In the fall of 2010, four friends and I gathered at a nice restaurant, together with our service and guide dogs, to enjoy a meal together. Besides my guide dog Cranberry and me, there was a woman in a large electric wheelchair and her service dog, another woman and her medical alert dog, and a husband and wife with their Guide Dog for the Blind puppy in training. We arrived before 6:00 p.m. and laughed and talked and ate until late in the evening. We were having a great time, enjoying delicious food and stimulating conversation; the hours went quickly by and it was time to leave.

When we departed, the woman in the electric wheelchair moved away from the table first. People who were dining at that time had not seen us arrive, so you could hear, throughout the restaurant, oh's and ah's and, "I never knew there was *a dog* under that table" as she headed toward the door. When the wheelchair user had moved away from the table, my guide dog, Cranberry, and I got up and made our way to the door. There were oh's and ah's and, again, "I didn't know there were *two* dogs under the table." The third to leave the table was the woman with the medical alert dog. More oh's and ah's and, "'How could there be *three* dogs under the table?" Last to leave was the couple with the puppy in training. The people sitting around us could not believe there was also a *puppy* under the table. He stole the show and the people just went head over heels when they saw this little fellow.

The five of us gathered in the parking lot before we all went our separate ways. We talked about how wonderfully behaved all these dogs were and how we loved it when the other diners didn't even know they were tucked quietly under our table. They were so pleasantly surprised. We had a great evening, all the dogs were perfect and the food was delicious—friends, dogs, food and fun, what could be better?

I would like to recognize my Cranberry – Certified Therapy Dog (yellow Lab guide dog) and Corey (Nova Scotia Duck Tolling Retriever)—without them this story would not be possible.

SECOND CHANCE by Christine Krivicich Cesarino

In September of 2009, I worked with the MOMS Rescue to adopt a shelter animal from Georgia. They were working on adopting out over 100 animals they had rescued from a shelter in Georgia to new families across the country. I saw Nala's picture on an email they passed around. I took one look at her sad eyes and instantly felt such a connection. I knew it was a sad backstory. MOMS told me Nala had been seized by the SPCA in Georgia from her home where she was being neglected and starved. She was turned into a crowded shelter with no real chance of adoption before MOMS rescued her. Wanting to give her a second chance at life, I sent her picture to my husband and asked him to make her one last wedding gift.

We were newlyweds looking to rescue a dog so that our shelter puppy, Stella, would have a playmate. We made the decision to take a chance on a dog we'd never met that we had only seen through a grainy picture.

Someone from the group drove Nala up from Georgia; we met them at the Vince Lombardi Service Station in New Jersey off the highway. After we got over our initial shock at her emaciated and run-down condition, with Nala's sweet disposition it was truly love at first sight! Nala required significant veterinary attention, a little rehab and socialization; but with lots of rest and love it has truly been the best decision we've made! I'll never forget watching Nala learn how to be a dog, from going up the

Nala, second chances do exist!

stairs for the first time to her first experience at the dog park to her finally trusting us enough to roll over for a belly rub. Not only are Stella and Nala an inseparable pair, but Nala is an incredibly sweet and loving dog and we swear she's grateful for her second chance at life!

A "J" LITTER PUPPY *by Joanna Meyers*

"Meyers!" the lady on stage called. My mother grabbed my hand and practically dragged me up there. I was in Oregon, more specifically at the Guide Dogs for the Blind campus. My mom and I were getting our first-time puppy, and all we knew was that it was a female black Labrador Retriever with her name starting with J. I was rather excited myself, but my mom was totally embarrassing me so I started grumbling about "controlling herself"— but the lady who was giving out the puppies cut me off.

That's when it really started to hit me—that after those long months of learning, seeing cute puppies, waiting and more waiting, it was finally here— I was going to get my own puppy to help socialize for Guide Dogs for the Blind. The lady on stage was now saying that "J" puppy's mom and dad were

Rumor (mom) and Marino (dad). Then she was saying what we already knew, "She is a female black Lab." As if on cue, up came the volunteer carrying our soon-to be-puppy. I then heard the announcer lady say, "This is....Jaunty!" as the volunteer passed Jaunty into my arms. She was good-sized for a female puppy and had a soft, glossy black coat. Her little pink tongue was lolling out, and she licked my face a little more than I would have liked, getting all of her drool on me. But I lived with it. My mom and I turned to the photographer to have our picture taken with our new friend.

That was a really fun day, getting Jaunty. I spent time with other puppy raisers, blind people, and most importantly a LOT of dogs. Raising a Guide Dog puppy has changed my life; it has opened doors to new friends, experiences and ideas. I know that when I give up my puppy, the one I love so much, I will miss her but also know that by doing this I am giving somebody a second chance to do things in life that they couldn't do with their blindness. I'm giving eyes. And trust me, those eyes see everything. Today, Jaunty is a happy five-month-old puppy and doing really well in her training. If all goes as planned, in a few months she will be leading a blind person, opening a door in their lives.

THE DOGMA OF LIFE *by Kathy Shaul*

I'm fortunate to be able to drive my daughter to high school most mornings. This year, since it's a short drive, we started bringing our dog, Hallie. Every morning at 7:30 a.m. when she hears the jingle of car keys, Hallie is exuberant and can barely contain her joy, trying to beat us through the door and be first to the car. This is repeated daily and never fails to make my daughter and I laugh. Life lesson? I think so. Dogs just "get it." They teach us every moment about relationships and how to live our lives, if we are only willing to notice and learn. When is the last time a ride in a car sent you over the moon?

Hallie, waiting patiently for her car ride

WOOKIE *by Chris Thomas*

Wookie came to us as a Christmas present from a daughter who had determined we were running low on dogs. He was a German Shepherd/Rottweiler mix and known as a "Shepweiler" on the card that

75

announced his arrival. Weeks later, if he was bad, he was then known as a "Rotterd." The reason we called him Wookie was because he looked much like the wookie copilot from the first Star Wars movie—a big, strong, friendly, hairy guy that would protect us.

We were in the process of moving to a small farm in the next state, so my wife was tasked with the eight-hour drive to our new place with the new dog and household stuff. Wookie stood behind her the whole trip, breathing into her ear. When she finally arrived at the new place, I had to leave because of my job. She was left that first night alone with the new dog, Wookie. He stared at her throughout the evening, and then finally, late at night, walked over to where she was sitting. He stood up on his back legs and put a paw on each shoulder and gazed into her eyes. She wasn't sure if this was the end of her, but all ended well—he dropped to the floor, relaxed and went to sleep. Boy, what a scary bonding.

Wookie was a tennis-ball-playing fiend. I would throw the ball as far as I could, he would take off like a rocket into the woods and shortly turn up with the ball. He liked to play to 200 but my arm was only good to about 50. I finally got an old tennis racket that saved my arm and kept Wookie happy.

Wookie had a sidekick called Ruby. Ruby was a dog only a mother could love. She was a junkyard dog—small, curly-tailed, somewhat ugly, a barker, and a general schemer. She continually got Wookie to chase anything. She would rush to the porch barking and carrying on, calling Wookie to join the chase, then be off. Wookie would charge off after her and Ruby would then reappear and take a spectator's seat to watch the coming drama. A deer would appear with a disgusted look on its face, then disappear. Shortly thereafter, Wookie would appear in full afterburner mode pursuing the deer, then disappear while Ruby was lounging on the porch congratulating herself on being clever.

Wookie had a favorite trick called "log moving." He would pick up a downed tree about 8 to 9 feet long and *Rubie, Gert, Chi-Chi, and Wookie* 3 to 4 inches diameter in the center so that he could balance it. He would then strut around, head and tail up, seeming to say, "Watch this!" He was doing this one day as I was talking to a neighbor who cut trees and sold them for pulpwood. Wookie came up behind me doing his log trick and ran the tree into the back of my knees—down I went—a nice football penalty clip. After seeing this trick, my neighbor wanted to borrow Wookie to collect hard-to-get logs for his business.

When Wookie died, he left a large hole in both our hearts. We will always remember what a great dog he was and how lucky we were to have him.

SUPER MADGE *by Belo Cipriani*

I had been walking for about five minutes up and down the numerous hallways when I heard a man offer me help. I told him where I needed to be and he said, "No problem! Should I write the directions down for your dog?" A loud laugh tumbled out of my mouth and I realized the stranger might not kidding when he began to talk to Madge, "Ok, puppy, just go down this hallway and make a left at the elevator."

Belo and Madge

The man had clearly knelt down as his voice sounded at Madge's head level. Interrupting the energetic voice, I pulled Madge closer to me and explained to the man that Madge and I were a team. "I give the directions and she guides me as safely as possible," I told the stranger. A big sigh came from the man who mentioned he was also heading toward the same direction and asked if he could walk with us. He continued to praise Madge for guiding me around some boxes, dodging a "Wet Floor" sign, and steering me away from the low-hanging branch from an indoor plant.

Guide Dogs for the Blind had teamed me up with Madge in 2009 and we had worked as a team ever since. Because I do not always catch every single small step or maneuver that she does in my favor, I realized I had taken some of her guide work for granted. We arrived at my dentist's office and I verbally thanked the stranger for walking with us and also mentally thanked him for narrating the obstacles Madge dodged to keep me harm-free. The man asked, "So, what is the hero's name?" Smiling and rubbing her velvety ears, I cheered, "Her name is Super Madge!"

DOWNWARD FACING DOG *by Belo Cipriani*

Madge and I arrived at the Yoga studio where we were welcomed by serene music, (possibly Enya). I asked the room, "Where do I sign up?" A calm voice answered, "Hi there, I'm so happy you're here. Will your dog be showing you the movements?" Assuming the woman was joking, I replied, "Absolutely! Her favorite pose is the downward-facing-dog." I chuckled and was startled when I heard this same woman cry, "Wow, that is great that she can do that for you." Before I could think of anything to say I heard the woman shout, "Tammy, come see this guide dog do Yoga." I announced to the room I was joking, but felt awkward when no one acknowledged my words; this was my queue letting me know the woman had walked away, and left me alone. Occasionally, I run into people who take anything I say too seriously. I think that it is hard for some to picture the blind being comical, sexy, or fun. Madge and I left the Yoga studio and walked down the street. I told Madge, "There is another Yoga place down the block; hopefully, they are a bunch of sillies— just like us."

DORIS IN TRAINING *by Barbara Edwards*

While on a camping trip to Oregon, we went to the market. As we were standing in line to check out, the woman in front of us kept backing up without looking. I was nervous she was going to step on Doris' tail, so I told my husband Jerry to get in front of me because the woman wasn't watching what she was doing. I guess the checker only heard bits and pieces of the conversation and had noticed the jacket on Doris so she asked if Doris was blind. We had to hold our breath to keep from laughing because the jacket clearly says Guide Dog for the Blind Puppy in Training.

Another time, we were sitting in a restaurant waiting to be seated. As usual, people always comment on how cute Doris is and then they start asking questions. We were talking to this one couple and the husband asked us if we have to pretend we are blind when we take Doris on outings. We said, "No, but when she goes back to Guide Dogs for professional training, the instructor will put a blindfold on her to experience how well the dog responds to the commands." It is amazing the number of perceptions people have about how service dogs are trained.

One of the funniest moments with Doris was when we were at the ophthalmologist's office waiting for my husband to finish his appointment. Doris was quietly lying by my feet when a woman came in and sat across from us. Immediately, Doris sat up and just watched the woman while we were talking about the GDB organization. The woman was amazed at how still Doris sat and just stared at her. I explained that she was waiting for me to give her the release to greet. The woman asked what the command was and I told her I couldn't say it because it was letters and Doris would respond. After a couple of minutes, I then gave Doris the "OK" and she immediately got up, wagging her tail vigorously as she greeted the lady. Everyone in the waiting room started laughing, including the staff.

CHAPTER TEN
Long Dog Tails

THETA CHI—DADS' WEEKEND – *From a dog's perspective*

Friday started off as a normal day—normal for any other dog, that is, but I am a guide dog and I have a different kind of "normal." I could feel that the sun was warm with a hint of spring and the birds were singing. Then I noticed that Clark, my master, was packing his suitcase. Not wanting to jump to any conclusions, I proceeded to speculate as he packed. As nosey as I am, when he went downstairs I had to follow. My tail began wagging as I saw him grabbing my travel bag. By now, all speculation had become concrete—ROAD TRIP! But where to I did not know and the mystery continued. I didn't think we had anything scheduled for this weekend so I just stood in front of him and stared at him with my head cocked to the side. He laughed and said, "Hang on, buddy, you'll know soon enough." I turned and headed toward the door—I never turn down the chance to embark on new adventures.

The car ride lasted about four hours and had us ending in McMinnville, Oregon. It was Dads' Weekend at my favorite boy's college in Linfield, Oregon and I was jazzed. I was wiggling in the back seat, staring out the window, tail wagging, feet dancing on the floorboards of the car as it came around the corner to Jacob's house. Not only was I going to get to see my buddy, Jacob (my big brother), but I was also going to see all of his friends as well as meet new friends. The best part of that is I get lots of "scritches." Note to self: Jacob has great friends!

Jacob showed Clark where our room was going to be and then let his roommates all say "hello" to me. By the way... they all love me. The house had my nose going into overdrive; I could smell the wonderful aromas of college living: pizza, burgers, T-bone steaks, ribs, smoked meats—wait a second; this is not food that normal college students eat. This was fabulous food and I wanted to take in every smell I could. But even better, everyone in Jacob's house played sports—there was the most amazing pile of shoes outside their front door—wonderful smelly shoes—I just love college houses.

We then headed to a restaurant with the two other dads that we had ridden down with: Jerry Nix, Billy Bob's dad, and Brit Shirey, Derek's dad. When we walked into the pizza parlor, my nose went into overdrive. Between Jacob's house, the campus, and the pizza parlor, I was lovin' the smells. Inside of the pizza parlor there was a cute little girl who approached me as I

Wonderful stinky shoes!!

reeled her in with my amazing stare that says, "Pet me, I know you want to," and I raised my eyebrows at her. BINGO...she got my master's attention, asked, and to my pleasure, he let her meet me and then pet me. Life is good.

After being a good boy and lying on the floor, I wasn't even rewarded with a dropped pizza crust—nothing, nada. To my disappointment, it was time to leave and head back to the Theta Chi Fraternity. Upon entering, there was music playing and odors my nostrils have never smelled before. A crowd of people meant it was time for me to turn on the charm and do some work. I

managed to do this in a huge way and, if my master had not had a tight hold on me, I might have just become the new mascot of Theta Chi.

As I came into the Fraternity, I noticed a morsel that was lying in the corner and I, being of K9 origin, thought this was would be a nice little snack. Well, you need to remember this is a guys' fraternity house. Normally I am not a finicky eater and it is not unusual for me to put all sorts of things in my mouth without even thinking—so I stretched as far as I could and snagged it off the ground—WRONG CHOICE! This crusty, old piece of bread might have been there for a couple of years—including a good amount of parasites from who knows what science experiment. Note to self: do not eat off a Fraternity floor! Not that they don't clean, but with a tongue like this, there is not much that I miss!

After a day of travel, smells, and people, I was definitely ready for a good night's rest, but then I found out that no one really rests on Dad's weekend. So even though I was not home, was in a strange town, and did not get to sleep with my boy on his mattress, I was happy to just be in his room with all of his smells around me!

Words of wisdom for my new Frat brothers - DO NOT EAT STALE BREAD OFF THE FRATERNITY FLOOR!! Eruff said.

"Wags to You" to Jacob's house family, Theta Chi, and all of my new friends!!! Arby

THE MOST FAMOUS DOG IN THOUMAN COUNTY *by Kathi Joye*

Forbes came to live with us on September 18, 2010. He was a Guide Dog Puppy in Training, four months old, and the focus of our son Keean's high school Senior Exit Project. Little did we know the impact he would have on our lives, our family, the high school populace and the small, rural communities in our mountain county. Through daily attendance at high school and regular visits to local businesses, Forbes endeared himself to everyone who met him with his charm, easy-going manner and his classic "So glad to see you" entire body wag. He was a quick favorite with my students at the local community college; nurses came running when he went to work with my husband in the ER, and local shop-keepers and patrons always kept their eye out for a "Forbes-sighting." Even today, I am

Forbes waiting for his diploma

not able to go into any business without someone coming up to say, "Hi Forbes,"—often I have no idea who they are.

It was at the high school, however, that he touched the most lives. Teachers, administrators and students looked for Forbes on campus to be met with his famous greeting, whether it was during the school day, at one of Keean's basketball games or any other after-school event. He was voted Winter Prom King by the student body in January. The administration went along with this but included Keean as a co-King. They then chose rally activities centered on dog themes. When May approached, we checked with the administration to see if Forbes would be able to walk in graduation with Keean; we were given a resounding "Yes." Decked out with a little black mortar board and orange stole along with his Guide Dog jacket, Forbes was one of the gang as they headed up to the football field for the opening march onto the grounds.

Seniors were allowed to express themselves as they walked down the runway to receive their diplomas; so, as Keean's name was called, he picked up Forbes and started to carry him down the path. As Keean approached the halfway point, the vice principal called Forbes's name and, immediately, the entire football stands of people erupted into a deafening roar. When he reached the end, Keean was handed his diploma, then Forbes received his own official high school diploma (with his name on it, too). As the crowd roared again, Forbes carried it carefully back to Keean's seat.

Forbes and Keean at graduation

I have had people approach me in the months since graduation when they see me with Forbes. They stop to tell me that they were at graduation and have never seen anything like it and never expect to again. They felt that Forbes clearly had become an important part of many lives here in Tuolumne County.

PARTNERSHIP *by Kelsey Mammen*

There's a rare stillness in the summer morning. The sun that will later pelt the earth with its heat is now just touching its feeble rays to the worn dirt of the hiking trail. I smile as the white blur of fur passes me again, intent on his upward path. "Keno!" I call as he surges a little too far up the path. He turns, bounding towards me in lip-flapping, Golden Retriever joy. As a puppy raiser of Guide Dogs for the Blind, it is a privilege to spend time with your puppies after you have given them up. Keno, unable to become a guide dog because of allergies, was spending some time with me before he goes to live with his adoptive family.

I'm pretty sure you are not supposed to pick favorites, but as I watch my fifth puppy, now a grown dog, bounding over logs and rocks, I can't help feeling that our souls are distinctly alike. There are few hikers on the route today so, for the most part, it is Keno and I. He races ahead, me keeping a steady cadence behind him. Only once do I have to encourage him to keep going when he feels something deceased needs to be inspected desperately and directly. We climb carefully, the dirt

Keno as he watches me

eventually turning to a loose rocky terrain. When Keno was a puppy, he was always on a leash in unfenced areas. In this moment, the uninhibited aura of freedom ripples through his body, throwing a smile on his doggy face.

As we get further from the parking lot, there are no human noises. Nature has encroached upon us, and the subtle creep of loneliness edges into my mind. We are alone, which is good and bad. Good for thinking, bad for dealing with the unexpected dangers of wilderness. As if he is reading my thoughts, Keno keeps closer to me. As the trail starts downward, it becomes steeper and rockier than the ascent has been. Keno changes his unabated running ahead. He still trots in front of me, scaling the sloping path much quicker than I. At the bottom of each rocky stretch, he stops, he sits, and he looks. He watches me as I slowly edge my way down, tracking my steps with his eyes. When my feet touch the point of evenness on the path, he is off again. He continues this repetitive behavior until I realize he is making sure I make it safely down every questionable spot. As we enter a small clearing, he looks back at me once more. Here he promises an innate partnership with his soft brown eyes, a knowing intelligence contained within their light.

JURY DUTY *by Grace Ehrman*

It was the end of January, 2009 when I had to report for jury duty at the Superior Court in Santa Ana, CA. I called my Guide Dog For The Blind leader and asked her what to do about the dog. She said, "Oh, Michelle took Madox when she had to report, and they wouldn't put her on a case because of the dog. So...Garden and I went off to the courthouse (we had to be there at 7:30 a.m. and Santa Ana is a good 30-minute drive). We checked in and sat with approximately three to four hundred people.

Garden

One of the first groups that got called was mine...these are people who don't work outside the home or are paid by their employer while they serve. The line formed and by the time we (Garden and I) got up to the window, she had all the people she needed for that case...so we went back and sat down. Not five minutes later, she called us all up there again. Well, we weren't so lucky this time. They sent approximately 125 people up to the 11th floor with numbers in our hands to report to the courtroom. Garden and I went in and sat in the back of the room where she could have a place to lie down next to me. I wasn't there but a few minutes when the bailiff came over and gruffly asked me if I had a problem seeing...??? I said, "NO, I am training this puppy for Guide Dogs for the Blind." In a curt tone, he said that he would have to go talk to the judge about this. Now, I thought I would be released and sent home. NO. He came back and asked me to take the seat right next to the exit door. So, I picked up all our gear and moved.

During this time the clerk called the numbers at random to come to the jury box. Well, guess who got called second? Yes, now Garden and I had to pick up all our stuff and report to the chair of Juror #2. After they filled the twelve seats of the jury, they asked their questions, first from the judge, then the attorneys. People were asked to step down, and more were brought for more and more questions—more and more people moved in and out. Garden and I stayed put in Chair #2. At the end of the first day, we were told to come back the next morning, but not till 8:30. That was a relief.

So, the trial finally began—a murder trial that lasted seven days. Every day Garden and I would come; everyone in the courthouse knew us by now. They all knew her name and that she was a Guide Dog for the Blind puppy in training. Everyone wanted to know more and more about Guide Dogs for the Blind and puppy-raising. The trial was finally over, and we went into deliberations. It didn't take us long to find him "guilty." But the funny part of the whole thing was that at the end, the same bailiff who was so curt and sharp with us that first day now came into the deliberation room and asked if Garden needed a break...

Garden now lives with a family in Northern California with three children. She runs with her master three miles a day and has a wonderful life. She didn't make it as a Guide Dog for the Blind because she has something called patellar luxation, a condition that means the kneecap can pop in and out of its joint. Wearing a heavy harness (which guide dogs do when working) could cause this condition to be detrimental to her abilities as a guide. So, she is now a wonderful family dog who loves life and loves her family.

RAISING EMMY *by Kimberly Harney*

In the fall of 2006 my roommate and I received my first baby Guide Dog puppy—a wrinkly, female, yellow Lab named Emmy. My roommate had raised the puppy's dad and we could not have been more excited to raise a puppy that we got to help name and would remind of us of her dad, Simon. I knew raising a Guide Dog puppy was going to be special. Emmy was an amazing puppy–I can't say that about every puppy! She was beautiful, sweet, cuddly, funny, and the most loyal dog I had ever had. She became my best pal and slept on the floor next to me most every night (Okay, we won't tell anyone that I occasionally woke up with a furry foot warmer). Emmy became the center of my world and had a

Kimberly and Emmy

following everywhere she went. Throughout her training she was an excellent ambassador for Guide Dogs and learned everything we threw at her like a pro. She was simply perfect.

In May of 2007, the day came where Emmy would go back to Guide Dogs for her formal training. This is when I realized how close Emmy and I had become and how the quick twenty-minute drive to the Guide Dog campus would forever feel like hours on the drive home. Dropping Emmy off that day, I left a large piece of my heart at Guide Dogs. For the next six months I would go to bed every night wishing my phone would ring to say that Emmy was coming home—I truly believed she belonged with me and would soon return home.

In October of 2007 we got word that Emmy was excelling in her training and my dream of her coming home was looking less realistic. Thanksgiving of that year I heard the words I had been praying I would never hear: "Emmy is in class to graduate." Heartbroken would be putting it mildly. How could a dog I put so much work in to be going to live with someone else? Who could possibly need Emmy more than I did? Who else would tattoo her name on their foot? That following week I got the answer to all of my questions when I got to speak with Emmy's new partner, Tim. Tim is from Missouri and is legally blind because of multiple sclerosis. Tim had fallen in love with Emmy in the short few weeks they had been together and in our short conversation I knew that Tim needed Emmy and that is why she would not be coming home.

Meeting Tim will forever be one of the hardest days of my life. My heart was breaking over a dog that I had become so attached to and never believed would leave. However, seeing her with Tim made me realize what all of our hard work was for and changed my feeling of heartbreak into a feeling of pride. Many of our friends and family came to see Emmy that day—everyone knew how special she was to me and what a hard day it would be for me. However, I made it through the day because of Tim. He loved her as much as I did and I knew she was going where she was meant to be. Emmy will forever be my "heart dog" and Tim will always be a part of my family. Tim and Emmy have an unbreakable bond and nothing in my life will ever compare to raising Emmy and seeing her bond with Tim.

We have raised 12 dogs since Emmy. All special in their own way, one (Emmy's half sister) came home to stay and I am thankful every day that she chose to stay with us. Raising guide dogs isn't just about potty training, following protocol and socializing puppies. It's a life-changing and heartbreaking job, but Emmy and Tim serve as my daily reminder that my heartache is nothing compared to the life-changing relationship these dogs form with their person.

PEPPERMINT, CHIFFON AND RIDER *by Susan Mooney*

It's a dog's life, and we love it! Guide dogs had been in our thoughts for quite awhile, even before we started actively raising puppies. I was born and raised in San Francisco, not far from the San Rafael campus. My mother-in-law was a volunteer at the Reading Room for the Blind in Salt Lake City, Utah, and we were always impressed with the dogs we met over the years. My husband and I retired from teaching in public schools only to find ourselves teaching in a whole different capacity. With the help of our seven- year-old retired racing greyhound, Doppler, we have sent two Guide Dog puppies on to further training. The three of us are currently raising our third Guide Dog puppy. The puppies have all been quick studies, each with their own lovable traits and even more lovable quirks. They've learned a great deal during their time with us, thanks to our wonderful puppy club leader, but they've taught us so much, too.

Peppermint, a female yellow Lab, was the first of our puppies. She was full of energy with an insatiable curiosity and a fascination with everyone and everything. Places like shopping malls, quaint coffee shops, restaurants and grocery stores were some of her favorite venues. She is now a working guide dog in British Columbia.

Chiffon, a female black Lab, was calmer and a real observer of the human condition. She loved watching people at restaurants. My husband and I joked that she was writing a blog

Peppermint meets Chiffon

about our neighborhood since she loved sitting in the front yard with us, watching the world go by. Chiffon had a special connection with children and spent many happy hours with me at the neighborhood school listening to kids read. She is currently in training at the Oregon Guide Dogs campus.

Now we have Ryder, a male black Lab. He's a real cuddle bunny and is crazy about our Greyhound. We know he can hardly wait until he's big enough to run in our yard with him. Ryder has just started his "official visits" but already he's prancing like a show dog in his jacket at the library and on brief grocery store visits.

All our puppies have taught us the value of living in the present, greeting the new day with enthusiasm as we get dressed for work, and looking for the good in every situation we encounter. Raising Guide Dogs and being involved with this amazing organization has given our lives a whole new dimension.

THE POWER OF GRADUATION *by Sherry T. Phillipsen*

The year was 1996 and our long-time neighbors and good friends had a wonderful daughter named Candace. She was an only child, but not the spoiled kind—just a wonderful girl. When she was 14 she decided to raise a puppy for Guide Dogs for the Blind. We were not familiar with the program, but Candace and her family gave us the five-minute version of raising a guide dog. We thought that was going to be very hard on Candace because she is a very sensitive girl— to raise a dog and then give it up. Over the next year and a half we saw Candace taking good care of the puppy. There were times when we were called to go next door and check on their puppy when the family was away from home for any long periods of time.

Our girls with Tanaka 2001

Eventually, the dog went back to the Guide Dog school and we didn't give it much thought. Months later we were invited to the Guide Dog Graduation Ceremony. Because they were such good neighbors and friends we felt honored and were happy to attend. At that time we had three young girls. I remember driving to the guide dog graduation and thinking to myself, "This is the craziest thing we have every done." It was a two-hour drive and it seemed crazy that they would have a graduation for a dog! We got to the San Rafael campus, and soon the graduation ceremony began. It was then that we realized this was much more than a dog graduation; this was a life-changing event for many people and many dogs. We watched in amazement at all the love, selflessness and acts of kindness. These dogs were changing the lives of everyone who was involved; from the puppy raisers, the Guide Dog staff and the recipient of the guide dog—not to mention the friends and family of those participating.

We were so proud of Candace! It was amazing to watch her give that little puppy that she had raised to a blind person. We spent the entire graduation in tears and we knew at that point someday we would raise Guide Dog puppies! It was 2001 when we received our first Puppy in Training, Tanaka. Our girls were older and the experience was very rewarding, not only for our daughter Erika (her raiser), but also for our entire family. Just as Candace had, Erika got to experience the same feeling one-and-a-half years later when she presented her puppy at the guide dog graduation. All three of our girls have since raised puppies and I am sure we will continue to be a part of this great organization for many years.

THE PORCH INCIDENT *by Chris Shafer*

"That dog wouldn't let me on the porch!" This came from my coworker, Pete, who had tried to set foot on my cabin's porch while I was at work. "I wanted to spray that hornet's nest above the front door but I couldn't get to it," he said. It was my third summer working at Priest Lake State Park as an interpreter, and my second summer working with Pete, a member of the maintenance crew. "Sorry, Pete," I replied, "I'll keep her indoors for you tomorrow."

According to Pete, Ellie, my Heeler-mix, had stood at the top of the porch steps with her teeth bared, steadily growling at him. She hadn't flinched. Fortunately, he had not persisted in approaching and had backed away. Ellie had never bitten anyone (well, outside of a herding nip or two). However, I knew that if she'd taken a stand like that, she'd meant business. Ellie did not bluff— she gave no empty threats. Over the years, she'd been in a few scraps with other dogs. The size of the dog didn't seem to matter; Ellie could hold her own with much bigger opponents.

Elli on the watch!

(Typically, she had been the one attacked and on the defense.) She was fearless in confrontations. Also, when it came to protecting me and/or my property, she took the "job" very seriously.

When Pete recounted the porch incident, a red flag warning went off in my head. Throughout the summer of 2002, a number of people had visited my cabin while I was away at work and all without any trouble from Ellie. I thought this over briefly and then dismissed the unpleasant encounter on the porch as a misunderstanding. After all, I'd worked with Pete for nearly two seasons by this time. I didn't see a problem with him. A few days later, Ellie was waiting in the car for me near the park's headquarters. As I came back to the car, Pete came by with a few guys from the maintenance crew. He tapped on the car window nearest Ellie and said, "There is that dog that doesn't like me." Ellie pressed her snout up to the window, curled her upper lip and revealed her long canine teeth. Her growl was low and menacing. She was ready to strike.

As I looked on, I was thankful for the glass between them. Seeing Ellie's strong reaction to this person was unsettling. My mind flashed to the porch encounter at my cabin. A cabin located in a remote part of the park, isolated. Not long after the porch and car confrontations, Pete was caught stealing campers' cash payments and was promptly fired. When I heard this I began looking at my dog differently.

I was in awe of Ellie's instincts. Apparently, she had smelled the rat in Pete. I told a friend about Ellie's behavior toward Pete and she replied that dogs could sniff out people with bad intentions. After the porch *square off*, I never second-guessed Ellie's warnings about people again. Most of the time, when it came to others, she was fairly indifferent; being a one-person-dog type—she didn't really seem to care much about other humans one way or the other. The few times that she got her hackles up after targeting Pete as unwelcome, I paid attention. While I tended to give people the benefit of the doubt, Ellie, on the other hand, was able to sense things about people, things not

Chris and Ellie

immediately apparent to me. From that summer on, my trust in her to protect me was complete. Her devotion to me was fierce, and I had no doubt that she would lay down her life for me. I never felt as safe as when she was by my side or on the porch.

JOSHUA FIT D' BATTLE *by D. Faye Higbee*

As the snowflakes lightly drape my back porch in a cold white blanket, I sip my coffee and remember one dog that I will miss until the day I pass from this earth. His name was Joshua. And he always "fit d'battle." He became a part of my "pack" when I dropped by the Safeway store in Sandpoint, Idaho to pick up something or another. (Don't remember what, by now). A friend and I had spent the day snooping through Sandpoint's eclectic mix of stores and restaurants and were ready to head home to Coeur d'Alene. At the entrance to the store was a large cardboard box manned by two young kids and an adult. Word to the wise—never, never, look inside a cardboard box at the grocery store—not unless you are prepared to add to your household some waif with four paws and fur. I thought it was a box full of bear cubs. Honestly. There were six black fur balls bigger than your average breadbox wrestling around in the milieu. Curiosity got me and I reached in the box. It was done before it started. One fat little critter wrapped his paws around my arm and literally would not let go. You'd have thought an octopus grabbed me. Then I foolishly looked into his deep brown eyes and turned to mush. I named him Joshua and we became fast friends.

Turns out they were Newfoundland-mix dogs. A Newfoundland is a dog, actually, not a bear, but they can fool people. As Joshua grew, he started to take up the entire back end of my Subaru, Justy. People would walk by the car and stare. "What's that in your car? Is that a bear?" It was a question that repeated itself incessantly for the entire twelve years of Josh's life. As a puppy, Joshua was fearless. He ate the first five books of my expensive leather Bible. A very spiritual dog, can't you tell? He also took on the lamp in my bedroom. After a huge battle, he managed to break the ceramic and jam the lampshade on his head. He sort of resembled a Chinese worker with one of those big round hats (except that he had a little trouble getting his bearings and staggered around the bedroom for a while before I managed to get it off his head).

Then there was the log chain caper. Joshua was an expert escape artist. He enjoyed visiting the neighbors. He jumped one neighbor's fence to play with their Golden Retriever, although getting out was another matter. He could jump a six-foot fence to get in the yard, but had no clue how to do it again to get out. The neighbors did not appreciate his escapades, by the way. He was also a master thief. The sight of a black ball of fluff bolting down our country road with an entire loaf of French bread stuck in his mouth was delightful. Well, except perhaps from the victim's point of view. He also seemed to enjoy stealing their throw rugs, boots, socks, and anything else left unattended. The neighbors threatened me often. Because of this I attempted to chain him up with a log chain. For the uninitiated, a log chain is so thick that it can usually only be broken with something like a cutting torch. Joshua managed it. He continued to escape until the day we moved to a new home. I hear the neighbors had a celebration that day. Joshua's battles included protecting his Mom (me). As a single woman, the dating game always seemed somewhat tedious. But Joshua was an expert at expressing his opinion. One man had the distinct honor of Joshua's lifted leg on his pants. Joshua bestowed a paw blessing upon another man by scratching him in the eye. He never let door-to-door salesmen return. One lunge against the screen door by a 135-pound bear cub convinced them to leave. I loved that dog.

Eventually I met Myron, the man who would become my husband. What would Joshua do? I opened the door and invited Myron inside the house. He sat on the edge of the couch, scratched Joshua's chin, and it was over. They hit it off and we got married. Joshua's final fight was against bone cancer. He had "fit d' battle" all of his life—but cancer was a battle he couldn't win. We'll never forget his endearing antics, fearless protection and loyal love.

A DOG OF QUESTIONABLE ANCESTRY *by Larry Laws*

During my pre-teen, milk cow wrangling days, I was fortunate enough to have a four-legged assistant complete with questionable motives. He could be a big help in keeping the cows lined out for home or he was, at times, responsible for a late milking. I firmly believe he and my riding bull could actually communicate. My degenerate hound had been incorrectly named Shep. A more fitting name that matched his whole makeup, however, was Alibi, and he always had one. To start with, he had a variety of distinguishing features, none of which would be claimed by any breefd of dog. Even with today's highly successful DNA testing, it is doubtful his lineage could have been traced very far back. The narrative for a "Heinz 57" would be the most descriptive.

Alibi had a habit of chasing anything that would run; and even some like porcupines and skunks that would not. Once he nearly lost a front foot while trying to bluff a badger. I couldn't find Mom's iodine but was fortunate enough to locate some turpentine. By his body language, it was easy to see his appreciation was strained but he didn't get an infection. His two main chores were to guard the occupants of the farm and help with the cattle wrangling. One morning before daylight, we were awakened by some yipping and yapping coming from the kitchen area. The kitchen and living room were in an L-shape with a window on the kitchen side and this seemed to be where the commotion was coming from. When Dad opened the window and stuck his head out to yell at the dog, he was greeted by a snap and snarl inches from his face. He shined the flashlight down directly in the face of a cornered coyote that old Alibi had rounded up. That was the signal for some protection duties, and he leapt on his enemy and got in a few bites before Wily Coyote got loose. A couple of days later, I found the remains of the chicken grabber out by the south fence, proving Alibi had counted coup. I had noticed his loose-lipped smirk and kind of wondered what he had been up to. I have to admit he did have a few good habits, but his ugly appearance dwarfed most of them.

After looking through Sis Ethel's picture albums, I realized I might have to rescind some of my assertions about Alibi's lineage. I located a picture of his alleged grandfather—being personally acquainted with his alleged father provided some serious speculation. Back in those days, canine birth records weren't kept. Also, neutering and spaying methods were only reserved for the city dwellers. With no older one yet alive in my family, I'll just have to rely on my memories of the neighbor stories of Alibi's two preceding generations. It appears on my memory screen that those neighbors related successful visits, a few years apart, by his grandfather Jack and father Pete. As I said, with no records for verification, I'll still maintain a possible questionable ancestry. Hearsay isn't always admissible. I couldn't find a picture of his alleged father, Pete, but by comparing Grandpa Jack and Alibi's photos, there is a strong family resemblance.

Alibi was a long, curly-haired mutt with a ring of fur around his neck that saved his life a few times. One time I became thoroughly ashamed of his matted fur characteristics and used Dad's horse shears in an attempt to make him into a facsimile slick-haired hound. Well, after much snapping, snarling, squirming, pinch-biting and utter lack of gratitude, I was running out of hair and had to quit trimming. I tried to explain to him that if he would have held still there wouldn't have been so many hairless spots on his tender hide. Thankfully, it was early in the season, so his ugly fur mat grew back by fall. We got along pretty well as long as the shears were held behind my back until l had a firm hold on him. I didn't deem it necessary to completely denude him again, but his eyebrows grew straight down and mixed up with his sideburns, inhibiting his eyesight. After hog-tying his legs, muzzling his pinch-biters and explaining how it wouldn't hurt much, I relieved him of some unnecessary blinders. Some of his derogatory innuendos were difficult to ignore until I thought about his unknown and questionable ancestry.

GROUCHY GRETA *by DuAnn Lustig-Chambers*
Greta pushed her four legs through the mounds of powdery snow. Not an easy task as she already had deeply imbedded snowballs lining all the fur of her legs and skirt. She waded deep, burying her beard and face completely with a series of muffled snorts and powder-filled breaths. Her black and silver cropped ear tips were all that were visible, like periscopes of a submarine emerging from the sea. "Whadja find down there—what?

Nothing to growl at?" asked her owner Anne with a giggle. Greta's small Schnauzer head popped out of the snow like a Jack- in- the- box dripping loose ice crystals. The white silhouette of her black body stood frozen in place, a pose of preemptive attack clearly readable despite the snow mounds that covered her.

It was the middle of December, this was her first snow experience, and she was loving every minute of it. Greta was a fun pup, full of all the happiness and playfulness that a baby Schnauzer offers. She was only eight months old and had more spunk than Anne had anticipated, but her grouchy side was a SERIOUS challenge! Greta growled and howled at everybody, using every octave possible. Whether she was happy or mad, she sounded like a grouch! Anne had tried everything she could think of to break the habit of her growling at people to say hello. It was not well received by her friends; or by anybody else, for that matter. Anne thought walking among strangers might desensitize her to the need to growl or, at the very least, desensitize the passersby to Greta's grouchy behavior. Anne hoped that eventually Greta would stop growling when she saw familiar people. It was an arduous task to train the growling and howling out of Greta, but Anne wasn't giving up! She wasn't going to own a mean dog!

"Grrrr," Greta growled as she sprang out of the snow and onto Anne's boot with the lightning-butt springs that Schnauzer s have. She took a mouthful of puffy snow pants between her teeth and started running, not getting in one full stride before losing her tooth-hold and rolling her snowballed body over on the walking trail. Anne laughed, delighted with Greta's puppy antics, reveling in this moment when her Schnauzer was acting exactly like a friendly and carefree Schnauzer should. Looking ahead on the trail, she saw the outline of two people walking toward them and her laughter morphed into a sigh. "And we'll try this again," thought Anne to herself, watching the approaching trekkers with hopefulness and worry, and not necessarily in that order. They continued along the freshly-plowed walking trail that lined the edge of the town. The trail was well liked by the townspeople, most of them being dog owners. Greta caught sight of the two strangers ahead, her little lips puckering to form a perfect "O," pulling her snow-encrusted whiskers forward like a bristle brush in front of her nose. An hourglass shape of Schnauzer stubble, as slim as a pencil lifted on her back—her hackling instinct, a well-developed. "Wooo" came from her mouth, a high sound somewhere between a growl, a purr and a yodel. She was already intensely protective, alerting Anne to the oncoming humans on their path.

"Okay, Greta, here's a chance to practice being a civilized dog. Can you try not to growl at them? They will tell you how cute you are, you know." Greta looked up at Anne from under her long speckled eyelashes overshadowed by silver eyebrows. A "knowing" older than her eight months flickered inside her eyes. Greta considered what Anne wanted, even DOUBLE-considering it...but she just COULDN'T do it. Her lips pursed, her ears pricked forward and the black ridge on her back stood at perfect attention. The strangers, now directly in front of them, noticed the developing snowballs fluxed into Greta's legs. "Oh, look at the snow in her legs! What a cute puppy!" said one of the women, eyes sparkling at Greta's baby body. "Is she nice?" The woman extended her fingers towards Greta's head and bent down.

"Drrrrrr, grrrrrr," growled Greta, watching them. She made no move to bite. The woman pulled her hand back quickly and stood up. "Oh, I guess not!" she exclaimed in surprise, taking a step back. Anne smoothed down Greta's freshly-hackled back explaining to the women that Greta growled at everybody when she was happy AND when she wasn't. The women looked at her unconvinced. "Really," said Anne trying to sound convincing, "she will let you hold her, but she will make those funny growl sounds in the beginning." Anne paused a minute trying not to sound as bewildered as she felt. "Do you want to hold her?" Anne asked, hoping that as more strangers handled Greta, the less her need would be to growl. Owning a growling puppy was SUCH an embarrassment! Thank goodness she didn't bite!

"Well, if you promise she won't bite," said the woman, looking at Greta wistfully. She cautiously reached her hand out to the puppy. Greta growled two octaves lower, but let the woman pick her up. Greta stretched her neck to smell the stranger's scent, completely covering the woman's nose with her silver beard. Anne held her breath, ready to lavish praise on her young pup. Was it possible that Greta was starting to develop some manners, she wondered hopefully.

"Drrrrrrrr, drrrrrrr," growled Greta softly, then paused and grunted twice, breathing in the woman's breath again. Greta arched up her nose to the sky and with her mouth forming a perfect "O" again, she howled and yodeled at the same time. The woman laughed and said, "Well, you definitely don't have trouble expressing yourself, do you? My name is Sally." Greta dropped her nose down, switching from her yodeling to a humming. "What do you call that?" asked Sally with a toothy smile, "Howldeling?" Anne burst out laughing. "Well, I have never put a name to that sound. Most people just think she's rude." The woman's companion piped in, "I don't think you have a growler here. I think Greta is a SINGER!" Greta, Anne and Sally turned their attention to Sally's friend. "Hi, Greta," she said, "I'm Lucy." Greta started in immediately with a medium octave yodel, "ldrlrlrlrlrlr, rrrrrrrrr." All the women laughed in unison. "You see?" said Lucy. She plucked Greta out of Sally's arms just to prove her point. Greta yodeled higher, and then dropped down to low holding tones. "You have a singerrrrrr!" sang Lucy in mimicking high and low tones. Lucy loosened the red scarf around her neck, cleared her throat dramatically and broke into the holiday song, "*Jingle Bells*." Everyone was surprised when Greta followed suit, not in words, but in sounds. Greta was able to mimic every note that Lucy sang, with her neck stretched long like a trombone and her little mouth pursed in her perfect "O" position. Anne was in utter shock. All this time, she thought she had a misfit grouchy grouch. She couldn't believe her ears. Her puppy was a singer!!! A GREAT singer in fact! She watched Greta as if seeing her for the first time. Her body sat quiet in Lucy's arms; only her little mouth and neck moved and twitched as she found each note, entirely focused on trilling in unison to Lucy. There she was singing along to "*Jingle Bells*," using all the sounds that Anne had heard over the last five months! Every last growl, howl, and purr that she had scolded Greta for repeatedly now sounded like a flock of angels singing praise in a strange and ethereal language.

The song ended and Greta was ready for more, so Lucy immediately started again with "*Silent Night*." Greta never skipped a beat or a note. She kept her neck stretched up towards the sky, trilling, growling, and yodeling with all her might, staying in perfect tune. A crowd began to gather from each side of the walking trail. In the few minutes that Greta and Lucy had been singing, several dozen adults and children had approached, forming a loose circle around them. Anne could hear people whispering to each other in amazement and pointing at the singing dog. And then, something even more amazing happened! A child's voice joined in with Greta and Lucy. It was a little girl's faint voice that was beautiful and pure and sweet. The crowd parted ever so quietly, revealing a girl, about five years old, bundled in winter clothes, her hands stuffed deeply into her coat pockets. She stood next to an older couple that were clutching each other and had begun to cry softly. The little girl only watched the puppy as she sang, unaware of anything else around her. The look of wistful sincerity on her face while she sang brought tears to Anne's eyes. She didn't know why. She only knew that she was witnessing a miracle.

The only being that the girl was even conscious of at that moment was Greta and her singing. Lucy beckoned the singing girl towards them with her hands. The little girl walked to them, standing next to Greta, singing softly. The crowd listened to the singing trio, mesmerized by the experience. At the end of the song, there was not a dry eye among them, except for Greta who carefully and efficiently shimmied herself into the little girl's arms, both of them completely unaware of her wet, snow-packed legs. Instead of growling and howling like she normally would when meeting someone new, she licked the little girl once from her chin to her eye, and stared into the little girl's eyes. "Hi. I'm Cassi and I like your singing," said the little girl to the dog.

The older couple that had been standing with Cassi rushed up and gave her a big teary hug. "I didn't know you could sing so beautifully!" said Cassi's grandmother. Greta gave Cassi another long kiss on the cheek, and jumped into Anne's arms. Greta did not make another sound. Cassi's grandparents continued to wipe away the tears that were pouring down their cheeks. "My granddaughter," she motioned to the girl, "lost her mother...my daughter," she paused to steady her voice and clutch her husband's hand, "just six weeks ago. Cassi hasn't spoken a word to anyone since then." The crowd gasped. Anne blinked twice, comprehending what had just transpired. Greta was quiet, and relaxed, ears perked forward. Cassi's grandfather wiped the tears off his cheeks and asked Anne, "How in the world did you train this dog to do such an incredible thing?" He put his arms around his granddaughter's shoulders, squeezing her tight to him. She looked up at him, smiling serenely for the first time since her mother had died. Anne took a step towards Cassi's grandfather, gulping back the knot in her throat. "Would you like to meet her? We call her 'Grouchy Greta'."

GOING UP! *by Shirley Douds*

I am Shirley Douds, a puppy raiser for Guide Dogs for the Blind. I would like to tell you a story about my Guide Dog puppy, Mojave (pronounced Mo Harvey). He is now a working guide dog in Arizona but I raised him near Seattle, Washington. One day I took my Guide Dog puppy, Mojave, to Seattle for a business appointment. Now let me tell you, he was a very handsome yellow Lab with the most strikingly beautiful eyes—and he knew it! It was a dull grey day and people were rushing to and fro with their heads down to avoid the cold damp wind. We entered the lobby of a busy skyscraper and found the elevator. The doors swooshed open and we entered with a group of professional-looking men in suits and ties. Mojave, who was quite comfortable with elevators, was perfectly composed next to me as the doors closed. "What a beautiful dog!" someone exclaimed. I heard this everywhere we went. All eyes gazed fondly at Mojave and he knew he was being admired. He sat there smugly and soaked it all in.

I never got tired of it, because puppy raising is dependent on the goodwill of the public and the businesses we visit. I said, "Thank you," and prepared myself to answer the usual questions: How old is your puppy? How long does it take to train him? When will he be with a blind person? Do you know who will get him? How can you give him up? I answered everyone's questions as best as I could while "Mister Confidence" sat there posing for them. He looked encouragingly into the eyes of each person who spoke. He seemed to say, "Yes, aren't I great! Tell me more." He gave the slightest flicker of his tail to each new question as if to say, "I know you are talking about ME! Do go on. Don't stop now." Then I noticed the elevator was not moving and asked, "Did

anyone press the button?" Stunned silence followed. All at once everyone realized we had been so enamored with Mojave that nobody had pressed the button to go up. We were all still standing in an elevator on the first floor being charmed by a loveable dog. There were fits of giggles and hoots of laughter at what had just happened. I think it brightened everyone's day because they all left the elevator with a spring in their steps and a smile on their faces.

Mojave - Mr. Confidence!

NOT A PILLOW PET *by Barbara K. Rostad*

"A Poodle? A 'pillow pet?' Are you serious?" Yes, he was serious. My husband, never allowed to have a dog as a child, fell in love with Poodles when we attended a dog show. The full-size Poodles, known as standards—tall, stately, elegantly poised to take prizes—particularly captured his imagination. I was far less enthusiastic. Prissy was the key word that came to mind when I thought of Poodles. I couldn't have been more wrong. Historically, Standard Poodles were bred in France as hunting dogs. An active outdoor life was their birthright. Miniatures came later followed by the toy Poodle and even the teacup size. But whatever size, I really wasn't interested. My husband persisted and soon we spotted an ad enticing us to go look at a family of Miniature Poodle puppies. There were six of them in an assortment of colors, all stumbling over each other in their eagerness to get acquainted with the newcomers; all, that is, except for the smallest one, who stayed huddled under the lawn chair afraid to meet us. Of course, you can see where this was headed and, yes, that's the one we took home.

Serious about our new role as parents of a Miniature Poodle puppy, apricot in color, we bought a book on dogs. Chapter One, titled "How to Pick a Puppy," offered two no-no's:

1. Don't get the runt of the litter.
2. Don't choose a puppy that seems afraid to meet people.

We'd had this dog for two days and already we had two strikes against us. Our next hurdle: choosing a name. My husband of one year recommended Bridget. All I could envision from this was a maid in a black and white uniform, frilly apron included. Quite possibly even a Playboy Playmate. No thanks. I offered a name reflective of her pale apricot color and her ancestry: Champagne. My mate's response was swift and certain: "I'm NOT,' he avowed, "Absolutely NOT going to the door and calling, 'Here, Champagne!'" Whatever other alternatives we put forth are now long forgotten, but at last we agreed that Suzette was a name acknowledging her heritage without calling up imagery of hired help and was suitable for hollering at the top of our lungs. Endowed with a name and showered with attention, Suzette worked her way into our lives in short order.

Suzette Babysits

When Suzette came to live with us we already had a cat plus her first litter of four new kittens. Gretel and her babies had been kept in a box in a spare bedroom during their early weeks but as they got older, they were given more freedom. Mothering was serious business to Gretel and she was with her kittens 24/7 for that first month. Venturing out of her more confined quarters, she was quite suspicious of the newest household member. At last, one day she went outdoors and was gone several hours. When she came home, she discovered a couple of her kittens were curled up with Suzette in the dog bed. A look of absolute horror filled her face as she stared, frozen, at this heart-stopping sight. Silently and with grim determination, she stalked over to the bed to investigate the condition of her precious babies. When it became apparent that they were napping contently and were not being abused by this canine intruder, she relaxed. From then on, kitten-sitting duties were routinely handed off to Suzette. She and Gretel remained close friends long after the kittens were given away.

Invariably, two faces, side-by-side atop the couch, stood parting the living room curtains to watch for our arrival home at day's end. And each day when we entered our front door into the living room, two handmade throw pillows that adorned our couch would be unceremoniously lying on the floor, as if to affirm our dog's disdain for them. Suzette and Gretel became playmates, too, though always at the cat's discretion. That is, except when, just like a couple of graduate students seeking cheap Friday night entertainment, we'd put them both in a huge cardboard box, laughing ourselves silly over their combined efforts to knock it over and escape.

Suzette had canine friends too—the most memorable a substantial-sized blue-eyed Alaskan Malamute with vivid markings. He was named Illini after our neighbors' allegiance to that Midwestern football team. Suzette and Illini would cavort on our unfenced lawns, the Poodle racing along, ears flapping, huge dog hot on her heels until she would wheel suddenly, coming about-face and turning on a dime. Her larger pal kept hurtling forward until he could negotiate a far slower, wider turn and the chase could begin again. None of this, of course, fit the "pillow pet" mold. But my first solid clue that Suzette was not ever going to conform to such an image emerged on a camping trip. She loved hiking and was happy sleeping in a tent. She liked exploring around the campsite, too. But like any lady, she also appreciated a good perfume. One afternoon she came back to the camp simply reeking. Her choice of cologne—*Eau d' Desiree d' Dead Fish*.

It wasn't until she was twelve that Suzette took up jogging. Such a pattern was remarkable not only because of her age but because it involved a whole new attachment. This dog, which had seen me through both death and divorce, was bonding with a new family member, my second husband. She jogged with him in the wee hours of the morning, even in the rain. And she discovered another new fragrance—*Sentimental Skunk*.

Snow Country

Not content to be left in the car for any reason if she could help it, she also soon took up cross-country skiing. This was a new adventure for both Suzette and me, spurred by the heritage of my Norwegian-born mate. Did she really have her own skis? No, this made it all the more amazing—for while we were gliding along a ski trail, this small dog had to keep pace on her own four legs. Her four legs often became snowballs as if she had a Poodle clip. In fact, we kept her in a puppy clip without the pom-poms except for her tail. But sticky snow gave her four very fancy white ones. Sometimes when she tired, she'd whine about the unfairness of her situation. Once, in a burst of compassion, my husband stuffed her in his backpack where, after looking briefly about, she promptly fell asleep. Once was all it took. This smart cookie soon began to whine earlier and earlier into the ski trips. Why walk when you could ride? Age, she concluded, should have its privileges!

And Baby Makes Five

When Suzette was around fourteen, ever-diminishing vision eventually left her blind. I watched in awe as she learned to find her way around our house by placing her nose against the wall and following it to the doorway she wanted. This ability to adapt!

A first-time mother when most of my friends were packing their kids off to college, I had begged Suzette and Gretel, each well into their teens, to live through my pregnancy and delivery—both complied. Even before our son Erik was born, Gretel could be found in the nursery rocking chair near the crib. After his arrival, Suzette, now sixteen, quickly discovered that if she could locate that infant seat on the floor, I was not far away. She would lie down near the baby, confident that her loved ones were close at hand. This little Poodle was many things: adventurous, affectionate, adaptive, but a pillow pet? Never!

THE MAULING OF BABY BEAR *by Kristi Lynn*

Our son and daughter-in-law surprised us with a "Build-A-Bear" baby bear that announced the birth of their first child. "Baby Bear," as we named her, wore a cute little Onesie that said, "Coming July 2012—Baby." They had given her to us in the fall of 2011 and little Baby Bear lived for the past year and a half in our front entryway sitting on a rocking chair. That is, until a day in the fall of 2012 when our daughter's dog, Dasher, had a little too much unattended time on his paws. Now you need to know that for dogs, Dasher is a very smart seven-month-old puppy, too smart to let anyone catch him in the act. He is full of energy, and mischief is always lurking behind his slightly cocked head as he stares at me with his big brown eyes. Being the mom or grandma to this ball of energy was a full-time job while my daughter was at work. I had already decided that I did not want a dog—I did not want a good dog, I did not want a bad dog, I certainly did not want a puppy, I most

Dasher the "not so" innocent!

definitely did not want a mischievous puppy, and I absolutely without a doubt did not want a mischievous, quiet, puppy!

One morning my husband was in his office taking a long-distance business call that required him to close the door to keep Dasher from dashing in and out. I was downstairs taking care of household items and as I came upstairs I realized that it was unusually quiet in the house—too quiet when you know Dasher is out and about. As I rounded the corner and my feet touched on the hardwood floor, I felt my "mother's intuition" kick in and readied myself.

Quietly, I stepped through the doorway and turned the corner into the foyer. I could not believe my eyes. Baby Bear was nowhere to be seen—all that was left was a shredded little white Onesie—that and a lot of white fluff that used to be Baby Bear! As I called out to Dasher, he came running around the corner looking up at me, head cocked ever so slightly as if to say, "I didn't do it."

I immediately scolded him and took him out back. As I opened up the slider, all I could see outside was my backyard covered with white floating fluff. I could hear the neighbors over the fence asking if anyone had seen their little white puppy, I thought, "Oh No! Is their little puppy all over our lawn?"

But then I realized that I was looking at Baby Bear's guts—her fluffy, white, floating innards!! Dasher had dragged Baby Bear outside, and Dasher, the "not so innocent" had literally shaken the stuffing right out of her. Surveying the mess, I saw a torn, partially-skinned, unstuffed bear and noticed something in the middle of the yard.

Baby Bear torn up with stuffing all over the place—evidence left behind that Dasher was guilty!

As I got closer, I was mortified to see Baby Bear's small stuffed heart! I looked at Dasher and said, "Oh Dasher, how could you maul Baby Bear?"

Although Dasher was in the doghouse, the good news is that I was able to repair Baby Bear—but the Onesie had seen its last days as a fashion statement. Baby Bear now lives safely locked inside a cedar chest. And Dasher? Well, Dasher continues to keep himself entertained and we never have a dull moment when he is around.

Baby Bear put back together again.
Sadly, the Onesie was too torn to repair.

RAISING A GUIDE DOG PUPPY IN TRAINING *by Susi Cherry*

In 1987, my daughter Cindy and I were in a local grocery store when we saw a woman pushing a shopping cart with a beautiful puppy by her side. Cindy was ten years old at the time and very shy, yet she mustered up the courage to ask the woman why she had a dog in the grocery store.

The woman explained that she was a Puppy Raiser for Guide Dogs for the Blind (GDB). She said that she was given an eight-weeks-old puppy and her job for the next sixteen to eighteen months was to socialize the puppy, teach it house manners, take it everywhere and expose it to all aspects of life. She said she had been to the bank, cleaners and dental office already that day, and now the grocery store.

"Mom, can we be Puppy Raisers?" Cindy squealed with an unexpected burst of excitement. "I'll help! I promise! I'll walk the dog! I'll feed the dog! I'll even brush the dog!" This reaction was so unlike my shy, reserved, timid daughter. Immediately, I was afraid of committing to something that I knew so little about. The commitment to an organization for a period of a year and a half was a huge undertaking. And there were so many concerns. How would we handle giving up the dog? What if the dog failed to become a guide? How would my daughter handle this disappointment? Would we have the time to invest in this project?

I had never met a guide dog user before and the thought about how guide dogs were trained had never crossed my mind. I just assumed that someone, somewhere, trained these dogs to do this amazing work.

When I saw the excitement on Cindy's face, I realized that this woman had sparked an interest in my daughter that was worthy of more consideration. But right now, in the grocery store, late in the afternoon, trying to complete my shopping for dinner, I needed to temper Cindy's excitement. I reminded her that this wasn't a dog that would become our pet. We would have to return this dog to the Guide Dog campus someday to be trained. Then, with A wisdom far beyond that of a ten-year-old child, Cindy just smiled and, in her purest of thoughts, said, "Mom, that's okay. It will help a blind person."

Cindy and I attended a puppy-raising meeting held at the nearby high school. We saw lots of dogs in a tennis court. Over 35 German Shepherds, Golden Retrievers and black and yellow Labradors! Great big 85 to 95-pounders down to little 10 to 12-pound puppies! The beauty of this scene was they were all getting along perfectly. Some of the dogs were romping and playing with dog toys, others were clinging to their puppy raisers, but most were just enjoying and exploring the company of the other dogs.

When it was time to begin the training, the puppy raisers leashed up their dogs and began to walk in a circle while a young boy on a skateboard tried to create a diversion. The screeching sounds of the abrupt swerving and skidding of the skateboard on the pavement caused many of the dogs to become edgy and apprehensive. I watched as the raisers, with the gentle guidance of the leash and a soothing voice, kept the dogs calm and focused.

All of a sudden, someone threw down a handful of kibble and some pieces of cheese and hotdog on the ground. My instant thought was that these dogs would be lunging at the food, scrambling and scraping their toenails on the pavement to be first at this culinary feast. After all, everyone knows how motivated Labradors and Golden Retrievers can be for food—but to my amazement, as the circle of puppy raisers with their dogs passed by this temptation on the ground, most of the dogs stayed focused and ignored the food. For those whose dogs hadn't yet learned this control, once again, the use of the gentle guidance of the leash and a soothing voice from the puppy raiser helped the dogs stay focused. Well, I was sold! I filled out the application and mailed it the very next day.

My husband Ray and I knew how lucky we were to have a home, good health, friends and family around us. We both came from families who had a strong background in volunteering and fundraising for charitable organizations. It seemed very natural to pass this on to our children, but we had never found the right cause that would excite the whole family. Raising a puppy for Guide Dogs for the Blind seemed like the perfect fit. We all loved dogs, and now Ray and I had the opportunity to show our children how to give back.

About six weeks later, I received the phone call to come to the campus of Guide Dogs for the Blind in San Rafael to pick up our new puppy.

We walked through a large set of doors into an open-air hallway of the kennel complex. Five banks of dog kennels lined both sides of the hallway, each capable of housing up to sixty dogs. The individual kennels had a temperature-controlled indoor area and a long, outdoor, covered run area housing two dogs per kennel.

Walking down the kennel hallway, we saw all of the dogs standing on their hind legs, with a symphony of their barking announcing our arrival as if to say, "Here comes the new puppy raiser!" The signs over the doorways directed us to our destination: The Kennel Kitchen.

The first thing I noticed as I entered this room was how clean and well organized it was. The stainless-steel-countered island in the center of the room, housing hundreds of shiny, clean stainless-steel dog bowls on the lower shelves, was a working surface for the kennel staff to prepare the many bowls of dog food at each meal. A woman walked in and began to prepare the bowls for the evening feeding. Measuring each bowl with the proper amount of dog food and adding water created an aroma that permeated throughout the kennels. Now the concerto of the dogs was escalating; they, too, could smell their impending meal and were "singing for their food."

The feelings of excitement and nervousness grew as we awaited the arrival of our first Guide Dog Puppy. Finally, the door at the rear of the room opened and Cindy's expression immediately changed. Her smile was a mile wide as a young man placed a small, black, furry, wiggly bundle into her outstretched arms. One look said it all! It was love at first sight! Instantly, this new puppy greeted Cindy with licks and tail wags. Cindy buried her head into the soft, plush fur of this young puppy. I, too, smiled as I took in the sweet flavor of its puppy breath and lowered my head to accept a sweet lick from the newest member of our family. My instincts were right on. They told me that we were heading in the right direction and that raising a puppy for Guide Dogs for the Blind would be a very good experience.

The young man told us that our puppy's name was Amba, pronounced "Ah" as if your doctor was examining your throat. My immediate thought was amusement! Can you say, "ComeAhmba?" So, we changed the pronunciation of her name to Amba; "A" as in "Apple."

While Cindy continued to cradle her new puppy, the man handed me Amba's leash and collar, a bag of dog food and a book entitled, "Puppy Raising Manual," with an 800 number on the front cover. I remember thinking that this was better than when I left the hospital after giving birth to my children. No one gave me a manual, let alone an 800 number for help.

Later that evening, as I sat with my family around the dinner table reviewing the manual with my husband and children, I emphasized the important issues. I explained that raising a Guide Dog wasn't just the walking, brushing and feeding of the dog. We had committed to the responsibility to care and maintain the safety of this dog, so my family agreed to add one more rule to the manual; "Never Let Go of the Leash!"

Cindy kept her promises! Each day she got up early to feed Amba. After school, she took Amba on long walks, and she brushed Amba so often that I thought we'd have the first bald Labrador Retriever!

I admit that in the early days of puppy raising, I didn't know the first thing about training a dog, but I knew I loved the relationship between a human and a dog. Soon, I recognized that this relationship was far more complex than just feeding, relieving and walking a dog. It was this mutual concept of the interdependence between a human and a dog that enticed me. That is why raising a puppy for Guide Dogs for the Blind seemed perfect for me. They provided me with all the tools necessary to train a dog, and I provided the patience, willingness to learn and, most importantly, the love.

One afternoon, the doorbell rang. There stood Cindy and Amba. Cindy's little blonde curls were sticking out, her bright blue eyes were shining and the rest was covered with mud! With her entire sixty-pound body coated in grime and a sheepish grin, Cindy said, "Mom, Amba saw a squirrel and she just took off, but I didn't break the rule! I didn't let go of the leash!"

Each week Cindy and I attended puppy raisers meetings and, with the help of our Puppy Raising leader, very soon Cindy and I became proficient at handling a growing dog. Once Amba had all of her inoculations, we ventured into the community to explore new experiences.

I remember taking Cindy and Amba to a parking garage that had multiple levels. Over and over, we hiked up and down the open stairway. Learning the skill of walking, not hopping or running the stairs was necessary to teach a dog who would become a guide dog. You see, the open stairway of a garage structure is a difficult maneuver for a dog. Being low to the ground, a dog only sees between the rungs of each stair tread and, as it climbs the stairs, it envisions danger below. After a few hours and endless trips up and down the stairs, Cindy finally achieved her goal. She had given Amba the confidence to execute this task with ease. Amba had mastered walking up and down the open stairways.

In the fall of 1987, I received a phone call from the head of the Puppy Raising Department asking me if Cindy would like to represent all the puppy raisers in the Guide Dog organization at a major fundraiser in December. This was quite an honor. Back in 1987, there were over 600 puppy raisers in the organization and Guide Dogs for the Blind had chosen my daughter.

For weeks prior to the event, after school each day, Cindy would take Amba into the backyard, giving me strict orders to stay inside the house. When I managed to peek through the living room window, I saw Cindy and Amba working together. With Amba leashed up by her side, Cindy was using the commands she'd been taught in the puppy raising meetings. With a confident correction, she would encourage Amba to pay attention and focus. At the young age of just four months old, Amba was easily distracted and didn't seem to have the maturity to master many of these new tasks. One day, weeks later, I saw that Amba was finally getting it! Cindy's patience with Amba was paying off. Amba was starting to understand and respond to Cindy's commands. Sit! Stay! Heel! and Take! I also recognized that in the early days of raising a Guide Dog puppy, Cindy, too, was changing. She was maturing, taking this role as Amba's puppy raiser very seriously.

The morning of the Holiday Luncheon, the weather was typical for early December. San Francisco was shrouded in a light fog, but by 11 o'clock the fog had lifted and cool clear air bathed the city. We drove to the St. Francis Hotel, standing regal on the corner in the heart of Union Square. This elegant hotel, built in the early 1900s, had become a time-honored tradition for Guide Dogs for the Blind's Holiday fundraiser. Socialites from all over the Bay Area came to the St. Francis Hotel to support this worthy cause.

From the gold-gilded crown molding to the huge crystal chandeliers, the St. Francis was San Francisco at its best—elegant and opulent. Amba, walking on Cindy's left side and wearing a festive red collar around her neck, calmly climbed the long, curved stairway to the mezzanine floor where we entered the Grand Ballroom. The tables were set with china and stemware, all glistening with the glow of the holidays. I distinctly remember the centerpieces; small, stuffed, plush puppies sat poking their heads out of gingerbread houses made in the shape of doghouses. Totally adorable and so appropriate for this Holiday Luncheon!

Sitting in the audience, enjoying my lunch with the other women at the table, I heard the Master of Ceremonies announce, "Please welcome Miss Cindy Cherry and her Guide Dog in Training, Amba." Cindy, wearing her new holiday dress with Amba on her left side, walked out onto what looked like a long runway, about sixty feet in length, six feet wide and four feet off the ground. Cindy stopped at the halfway mark. With the audience sitting quietly in order to hear Cindy's voice, we heard the words "Sit! Stay!" Amba sat perfectly. And then Cindy did the unthinkable! She dropped the leash!

My heart dropped too!

Cindy turned her back on her dog, walked to the end of the runway, faced her puppy and gave Amba the command, "Heel!" Looking around, I saw that the audience was holding their breath, wondering what would happen next. Amba immediately reached out, picked up her leash in her mouth and, holding her tail high, strutted straight down the center of the runway, taking her place by Cindy's left side. This was an amazing feat for a four-month-old puppy. I wasn't the only one that knew this. The entire audience knew this. They began to cheer and applaud. It seemed as though the clapping would never stop. Then I heard this strange clicking sound around me. I asked the woman seated next to me about the sound. She just smiled and laughed. She reminded me that Guide Dogs for the Blind did not receive any State or Federal funding. It was only supported by private gifts. The clicking I was hearing was the sound of the women opening their purses.

After welcoming in the New Year of 1988, Cindy and I looked forward to the time when we could resume taking Amba on outings with our puppy raising group. Sometimes our group would take field trips with our puppies into the local mall, up and down the elevators, and in and out of all the stores. Other times, we would take our dogs on BART (Bay Area Rapid Transit) into San Francisco to explore Chinatown or Fisherman's Wharf. One time our group went into a McDonald's with seventeen dogs and had them sit quietly by our side to teach them to leave the French fries on the floor!

While Cindy was in school, I was the one responsible for Amba. She accompanied me everywhere. She became my special partner. Although Cindy and I co-shared the official title as Amba's puppy raisers, I often told potential puppy raising parents that it is usually 50% child effort and 150% parent effort. After all, kids are just kids.

That said, when I was given the responsibility of raising Amba, "The Guide Dog Way," I found it worked for me. When I was growing up, my family had a dog, or so it was called (as my eyes are rolling with a look of disgust). Jojo was a miniature Poodle, always sick, with back problems that resulted in him having to be confined to a playpen and being fed a soft diet of cooked chicken and dog treats. This wasn't my idea of a dog. Where was the Lassie-type dog that would romp and play rambunctiously with kids? I yearned for that type of dog. As we became familiar with the GDB method of raising a dog, I found that Amba could be rambunctious and playful and then, when leashed up, she would transform into a calm and focused dog. All it took was patience, consistency and more patience!

From the day we received her, Amba exuded a humanlike quality unlike any other dog I had ever had before. As we grew closer in our bond, I noticed she became in tune with me, able to read my mind and anticipate my every mood. At times, she was smarter than I was, often trying to circumvent the rules of her training, pulling and tugging on the leash, darting after squirrels instead of walking calmly by my side. The manual was valuable, with great tips and instruction about housebreaking, leash corrections and positive praise; but the advice of our puppy raising leader and other experienced raisers in our group was worth its weight in dog treats. As I learned the ropes of puppy raising and became the Alpha, the dominant figure in our partnership, Amba, too, learned and respected her role as my dog. This respect was so essential for her to learn if she was to become a Guide Dog.

My life changed in other ways too. I found that I needed to adjust my daily schedule. A simple trip to the grocery store with Amba took twice as long. Everyone was interested in her. What's her name? How old is she? How much does she weigh? As I patiently answered these questions, I realized that having a cute puppy by my side was not just about raising a dog for Guide Dogs for the Blind; it was all about the dog. It was about this unfamiliar scene of a seeing a puppy in a store or a restaurant, wearing a bright green jacket, announcing that she was a Guide Dog Puppy in Training. It was all about the dog whose job it was to learn to walk calmly and stay quiet—behaviors that were necessary to become a Guide Dog.

People were always asking me questions about Guide Dogs for the Blind. Where were the dogs trained? How long does it take? How much do the blind individuals pay for the dog? I loved answering these questions. With pride, I would tell them that Guide Dogs for the Blind has never charged a person for any of their services. Not for the transportation to and from the campus; not for the training or the dog; not for the harness or the follow-up services or even the vet care support. All of these services are entirely free.

I recognized the need to educate people about Guide Dogs for the Blind. Soon, I was giving programs about puppy raising to school-aged children. Over time, my programs expanded to women's groups, service organizations, churches and synagogues—to anyone who would listen to me. Educating people about Guide Dogs and Puppy Raising was extremely rewarding, yet I found that I was learning and experiencing life with a dog in a whole new light.

I remember taking Amba with me to my dental appointment. Upon entering the office, instantly Amba's body language told me something was wrong. Immediately her body stiffened, her tail wasn't wagging as it did when she usually greeted strangers, and her fur began to show a small amount of flakiness. She was definitely stressed. It was quite a challenge to get Amba to sit in the corner of the operatory. She wanted to be seated next to me, on my left side as we had taught her during her training, but this wasn't the safest or most convenient place for her to lie while I was in the chair. With my encouragement to ease her stress, she finally settled and took her place in the corner of the room.

I tried to imagine what Amba was thinking. "Who are these people with masks on their faces and plastic coverings on their hands? What was that noxious odor? And why were they hovering over my Mama with a high-pitched sound of whirling and whistling coming from her mouth?"

As the dentist began to drill away at an old filling, bits of dust particles and water spray began to fill the air. Immediately, with a sense of urgency, Amba stood up and came to my side and began to lick my hand. This endearing show of affection was unusual for Amba, because as part of her training she was taught not to lick; but right then I realized what Amba was thinking. "Are they hurting my Mama? Is she on fire? Does she need my protection?" This experience in the dental office was a new beginning for me. It was the first time I recognized that Amba and I were both beginning to think as a team. We began to look out for each other. I looked out for her, cared for her needs, and she was beginning to look out for me. After I relayed this experience to my puppy raising leader, she smiled and commented that Amba seems to have the right temperament needed for guide work.

The year and a half we had with Amba flew by far too quickly. As I collected the mail on a rainy afternoon in late December of 1988, instantly my heart raced and ached at the same time. Recognizing the return address in the upper left hand corner on the envelope, tears welled up in my eyes. The postmark was San Rafael, CA. I knew what was in the envelope. It was the recall notice—the notice telling me the date to return Amba back to the Guide Dog campus for her final six months of formal training.

My thoughts were whirling like a tornado! Didn't they know? Didn't they know that I wasn't ready to give up my girl? My Amba! I still had so many things to teach her, so many things to show her, and to share with her. Didn't they know I wasn't ready to part with her? When I told Cindy that we would need to return Amba, she bravely smiled and said, "Mom we've done our best. Now it is up to Amba to show the trainers "her stuff."

The evening before taking Amba back to the Guide Dog campus, Cindy and I sat on her bed, with Amba between us, nudging us for a belly rub. We reminisced about all the wonderful times we had experienced with Amba over the last year and a half. We laughed about the first time we took Amba into a newly-opened Vietnamese restaurant, and the waiter wanted to take her into the kitchen. We laughed so hard that we cried as we recalled our thoughts of possibly being served "Slab of Lab" smothered in "Bone-Suck'in Sauce."

That night I presented Cindy with a life-sized, stuffed black Labrador, which she immediately named Amba 2. Although I knew that this present was not a substitute for the real Amba, I wanted it to be a reminder of the time she had been a Puppy Raiser for Guide Dogs for the Blind and had raised Amba. In our private ceremony on her bed, we removed Amba's collar off from her neck and placed it on the neck of Amba 2.

While readying ourselves on the morning of Recall Day for the trip to San Rafael, Cindy confidently said, "Don't worry, Mom! I promised you. I won't cry. I'll stay strong!" But as I drove to the campus, I glanced into the back seat and saw Cindy staring out the car window. I realized that this was just a front for what she was really feeling. With Amba's head on Cindy's lap, our trip back to Guide Dogs was a silent struggle for her. Then I heard it. She couldn't hold her emotions in anymore. Sounds of small little sniffles that turned into cries of sadness began to fill the car. I knew what she was thinking. She was losing her best friend, a friend who loved her unconditionally, a friend who greeted her each day when she arrived home from school, a friend who she could tell her secrets to without fear of betrayal. I knew how Cindy felt, because I felt the same way too.

As we crossed the San Rafael Bridge, I remember the tears streaming down my face. Although I thought that we had prepared for this day and understood the emotions that we might experience when we would have to take Amba back to the kennels, a flood of thoughts rushed through my head. How were we going to live without our puppy? She had gone everywhere with our family! She was a part of our family! But we had planned for this day. We had talked about it often and we had already signed up for our new puppy.

In the kennel kitchen on the Guide Dog campus, Cindy, Amba and I gathered with other puppy raisers who were also returning their dogs for training. We all waited quietly for the trainers to come. Our faces told the same story. Some of the puppy raisers had quivering lips, desperately trying to hold back the tears, while others couldn't refrain so they just let their emotions burst out in an explosion of sobs. Although the moment was so intensely private, we were all experiencing the same feeling—a feeling of mourning or loss. As I was standing next to Cindy with my arm around her shoulder and Amba seated at our feet, we began to cry from the heartbreak of knowing that our dog would no longer be ours. Then my daughter, who somehow found some strength, said to me, "Don't be sad, Mom. Amba's going to become a Guide Dog!"

The door of the kennel kitchen swung open. Four trainers stood at the entrance. Three women and one man entered. The tall man, touting a black mustache and wearing a shirt with the Guide Dog logo on it, introduced himself as Amba's trainer. He walked up to Amba, held out his hand and offered her a bit of kibble as he ruffled the fur on her head. "Good to meet you, Amba!" he said in a warm confident voice. Amba's tail began to wag. It began to wag faster and faster and then, with accelerated speed, Amba's tail began to rotate like the propeller of a helicopter, all the while her feet were dancing and barely touching the ground. We had seen this energy before and called it the Amba Circle-Tail! Amba's exuberant attitude said, "Hi there! Are you going to play with me? Are you going to feed me? Are you going to be my new best friend?"

At that moment, we realized that Amba would be fine. She would be loved and cared for by the trainers at Guide Dogs. I remember thinking that Amba was like Cindy when she left to attend a summer camp for the first time. Like Cindy, Amba was wide-eyed, excited and ready for her new adventure.

The time had come. I bent down and gave Amba a long bear hug good-bye and whispered words of encouragement in her ear, "Don't pull too hard, Girl! Remember to stay focused!" Cindy smothered Amba with kisses on her cheek, bid her farewell and said, "See you at graduation!"

As the trainer walked Amba down the concrete hallway of the kennels, the other dogs in the training kennels began to bark, as if to say, "Welcome!

You've come to the right place! The food here is great!" As she was led to the doorway of kennel 4, which would now become her home for the next five months, Amba stopped and turned to look at us. Then, slowly her tail began to wag at as though she was conveying a special message to us. "Thank you for playing with me. Thank you for loving me! Thank you for being my Mama."

Amba's new-found spirit allowed us to smile and beam with pride as she departed from our lives to begin her new chapter toward becoming a guide dog. In our hearts, we knew we would miss this bundle of furry energy, but deep down in our souls we knew her purpose and we prayed for her success.

Knowing that Amba would be loved and cared for during her training finally gave Cindy and me permission to breathe easier. We now needed to regroup our emotions and focus our attention on our next challenge; a new, sweet, eight-week-old Labrador puppy named Brit. Can you say, "Brit, Sit!"?

Beautiful, black and bouncy, Brit renewed our spirits. Our tears instantly dried and ear-to-ear smiles filled our faces. Once again the smell of puppy breath bathed my heart. It was as though it was springtime and we were experiencing life anew.

The great part about raising Brit was that we continued to attend our puppy raising meetings. We would pay close attention to the part of the meeting where the leader read the progress reports about all the dogs in training.

Back in the 1980s, the formal training was a ten-phase program over a five-month period done by Guide Dogs' certified trainers. As the weeks passed, our puppy raising leader would announce "Amba, Phase 1," "Amba, Phase 2," "Phase 3," and then finally, months later, we heard "Amba Phase 10, Class Ready." This meant that Amba was going to become a Guide Dog.

Twenty-eight days later, with our family and friends, we went to the Guide Dog campus in San Rafael for the graduation ceremony. Cindy and I went into the dorm to meet the person who had been partnered with Amba. At the end of the hallway stood a young woman with a beautiful, big, black Labrador by her side. I recognized the twinkle in that dog's eyes. It was our Amba! All grown up! All mature! The woman bent down and took off Amba's harness and said four magical words, "Go see your Mama!" With that, Amba raced down the hallway and greeted us with licks and tail wags. She remembered us after six long months!

At this Guide Dog graduation, the real pomp and circumstance was not the presentation of a paper diploma but the moment that Cindy passed Amba's leash to the young woman. Immediately, we could see Amba's excitement as she saw her new handler. Once again, the movement of her tail spoke for Amba. This Circle-Tail action was Amba's fast-moving, circular rotating tail signature that demonstrated to all who witnessed it that Amba was over the top with joy.

Cindy found the courage to share with the audience her personal thoughts of the past two years. Standing in front of a crowd of about 150 people, in her small, now confident voice, my now twelve-year-old daughter spoke eloquently about how much she loved her dog and enjoyed the experienced of raising a Guide Dog.

As her mother, I smiled with pride and recognized that just two years earlier Cindy had been a shy, timid, fearful, young girl. Now, having had the opportunity to raise Amba and gain the confidence to speak to people about Guide Dogs for the Blind's Puppy Raising Program, Cindy had blossomed and bloomed.

When it was my turn to speak on the graduation stage that afternoon, once again, tears streamed down my face, but this time they were tears of joy!

I shared with the audience my thoughts of how my decision to become a volunteer for Guide Dogs for the Blind proved to be the right choice.

It was a win for everyone!

I won!

My time with Amba was a journey filled with joys and tears that changed my life forever. I was able to experience a unique human-canine relationship unlike any other I had ever experienced before. I also was able to show my family how important it was to give back to others.

Cindy won!

Cindy was no longer the shy, timid, little girl. She could now speak to people with confidence and ease.

Amba won!

Amba was now a trained guide dog, going to live in a loving home.

And Tracy won!

Tracy was a twenty-eight-year-old woman from New Jersey. She traveled each workday into Manhattan, taking two subways and a bus. Now with Amba by her side, she could travel safely and confidently.

The week after graduation, Tracy called me. She told me that her flight home was uneventful. She said she and Amba walked onto the plane, sat down and Amba curled up by her feet and slept the entire trip. But upon arrival, Tracy said things changed. She told me she grabbed the harness handle, walked through the jet-way into the crowded airport and realized that she hadn't asked anyone for assistance. She said she didn't worry about bumping into small children or stumbling over pieces of luggage with her cane. Tracy told me she loved the feeling as Amba wove a pathway through the crowded airport terminal. She said she'd even slowed down to listen to the comments about how beautiful her dog was.

Then Tracy's voice changed. I could hear the tears in her words. Tracy said that for the first time ever, she was no longer afraid. She said having Amba by her side gave her the confidence, the independence and the peace of mind knowing that she would be safe.

I thought that Tracy was the real winner of the grand prize, but here I am, some twenty years later, still volunteering with Guide Dogs for the Blind, giving speeches and tours and helping with fundraising. I realize that maybe I was the biggest winner. This experience has enriched my life, to the point of passion, thus allowing me to pass on the value of giving to others.

Who would have thought that a trip to the grocery store would make a difference in so many lives?

CHAPTER ELEVEN
Coming Full Circle

Saturday morning, Mother's Day weekend of 2012, would find me waking up in Coeur d'Alene, Idaho at my sister and brother-in-law's home. I was roused from sleep by the rich smell of sausage and eggs wafting up the staircase and the deep aroma of freshly-brewed coffee. Through the open window, I could hear birds singing a song to the rising sun and the slight hum of a semi truck's brakes from the not-too-distant freeway. As I felt the warmth of my blankets and the soft comfort of the bed, I closed my eyes one more time to try to recapture the deep, almost toxic last moments of sleep. Down on the floor, I could hear a quiet whine and could not only hear but feel the vibration of the thump, thump, thumping of Arby's tail. Sleep would have to wait until that night. With daytime and nature both calling, I pulled myself out of bed, threw on some clothes and went out to greet the day.

As I grabbed a cup of coffee and stepped into the warmth of the sun out on the back deck, I could hear Arby lopping in behind me. This was a special time of the day as the house was still asleep and the adults were able to just sit and visit. Arby was at my feet. Cody, my sister-in-law's dog, was trying desperately to get him to play, but Arby was enjoying this morning as well. I love the early morning as it is still somewhat cool, the sun is just beginning to warm up the earth, birds are playfully darting in and out of the trees, and somewhere in the back yard there's the melodic cooing of a mourning dove. I could hear the ticka, ticka, ticka of the sprinklers in the back yard and I allowed my brain to just roll on autopilot, freewheeling and spinning in many directions, not focusing on anything serious but just enjoying the moment.

The ringing of a cell phone came creeping in and my thoughts returned to the back deck and Arby. It was not long before my wife Karrie came out to let me know she had just gotten off the phone with her sister Kristi who had called to talk about Lacey, my 15-year-old retired Guide Dog. Karrie and our daughter Becca were in Coeur d'Alene to attend a Mother's Day brunch with her sisters, her mom, cousins and aunts. Definitely not a guy's weekend, but I had come along to keep her company on the road. Kristi was unaware that I was in town and she had wanted to talk to Karrie about Lacey's declining health. Kristi and Jerry (my brother-in-law) wanted to take Lacey to the vet that day to have her evaluated, but there were none open. This was a difficult time for their family as they had just recently lost their dog of fourteen years.

The decision of what was to come was weighing heavily on Kristi. She was feeling the heavy burden of responsibility and did not feel prepared to make it.

As Karrie and Kristi talked, Karrie told her that I was in town and that with everything that their family was going through, I would be very willing to ease the burden of decisions for these possible final days of Lacey's journey here on earth. Kristi sounded relieved and Karrie reassured her that they had done all that they could. Their family had given Lacey more than we could have ever hoped for in her retirement; love, attention, care, warmth of a home and a little Schnauzer buddy, Rocky, as a playmate. The past four years they had provided a wonderful life for her retirement and now it was time for me to step in and help Lacey come full circle.

As the day progressed, the ladies went to their luncheon and I hung out with my nephew Austin, helping him to man a homemade lemonade stand on a beautiful sunny, Saturday afternoon. In spite of the constant flow of people purchasing lemonade to quench their thirst, my mind kept wandering back to when I had received Lacey: The day she and I met for the first time at Guide Dogs for the Blind. Hugging on her, feeling her wiggle and lick my face as she said "hello" to her new owner. Hearing stories from Rand, her puppy raiser, about her first flight and how she had over 150,000 air miles before I got her. Flying home and watching in amazement as she just backed herself under the plane seat and curled into a little ball as if to say, "Piece of cake." The day she met Karrie and Jacob, Having Lacey share the role of flower girl with Karrie's niece Janaye and become the flower dog in our wedding. Watching as Lacey and Jacob became fast friends and best buds, and being so thankful that she was the "glue" in our new family. A boy and his dog—there is truly nothing like it! Yes, my mind was running down memory lane with Lacey by my side.

As we started toward Kristi and Jerry's, I decided to leave Arby at the house. I wanted to have this time with Lacey so that I could evaluate her and not have her or myself distracted by Arby. See, what you need to know is that ever since I left her in Coeur d'Alene she has ...well, for lack of a better word, she has snubbed me! For the past four years, any time I would come to visit Lacey (with or without Arby, my current guide dog), she would not give me the time of day. She would go to Karrie and the kids but she would turn a cold shoulder, nose and with a wave of her tail turn her back on me. Karrie said it was funny to watch. She would take a look at me or at Arby and turn away. As if to say, "You gave me away. You didn't need me or want me anymore so I am not going to talk to you or show you that I miss you." For the most part, that is how it had been for the past four years.

Upon reaching the house and entering the kitchen where Lacey was, she came right to me. She wagged her tail (which had not been working very well) as I took my hands and gently worked them over her entire body, evaluating her head, neck, muscle tone, legs, hips, and it basically allowed me to see her completely. I looked at her hips, seeing how slim she had become (just since the last month when we were here) and then I got down and was kneeling on the floor at face level with her. At that moment, she went nose to nose with me. Almost as if to say, "Where, oh where have you been? Why did you give me away? I am ready to go for a ride so where are we going and when are we going to leave?" Karrie said that she had a look of sadness, tiredness, and of gentle longing as she stood there allowing me to see her with my hands. Both Karrie and her sister Kristi stood in tears at what they were seeing; they could not believe how she was reacting to me. It was apparent to all of us that we had come full circle. It was time to go home.

Lacey and Clark - 5/12/12

After checking her out and knowing that we would not be able to see a vet in Coeur d'Alene, I made the decision to bring her home with us, back to Bellevue so that my vet could take a look at her. Lacey was suffering from many of the ailments dogs get as they get older; after all, Lacey had just turned fifteen and had enjoyed a wonderful long life. Her hips were giving her trouble, giving out on her and not allowing her the strength or control to stand up and lie down. She was having challenges with incontinence (bladder issues). A few days prior she had really stopped taking any significant amounts of food and over the last month she had lost a noticeable amount of weight. Her beautiful black coat had lost its luster and was no longer shiny, the pep was gone from her step, and her soft dark eyes no longer sparkled with eager anticipation to please her people.

With the decision made, all of the family was told that this would be Lacey's last trip. I would return back to Karrie's younger sister's house and break the news to all of the cousins as to what was happening. I tried to reassure them all that we did not know for sure what the next step would be but that we had to realize this would probably be Lacey's last road trip. The kids had all grown up with Lacey and she had shared their lives very closely over the past four years. It was very emotional and tears were shed, loves and "skritches" were given and goodbyes were said. The plan would be for Lacey to have one last night at her current home and then we would pick her up Sunday morning for our journey back to Seattle.

As I lay in bed that night, I tossed and turned and was in and out of sleep. I had never gone full circle with any of my Guide Dogs—the emotions in me knew where we were heading, but I was having a hard time believing it. This would be Lacey's last road trip. Beginning her journey as a puppy at Guide Dogs for the Blind, then off to her raiser's home, spending a year and a half traveling on every type of transportation you can imagine: car, bus, light rail,

ferry boat, and airplanes. Lacey had attended corporate meetings, met Bill Gates in his home, and had ridden in an elevator with President and Mrs. Clinton. Then after going back to Guide Dogs for her final training, she was partnered up with me, and spent the next 10 years speaking to thousands of children and adults before retiring. Now, returning home, she had come full circle.

Morning arrived and we were met with the news that Lacey was no longer able to get up on her own; she seemed to have taken a turn for the worse. The short car ride felt heavy with the knowledge of what we knew was coming.

Becca and Lacey spend more girl time

The family met us outside of the house, evidence of tears apparent on everyone's face. This was an emotional time for all, but especially for Jerry, Kristi and their family who had invested so much of their hearts and their lives into Lacey the past four years and had also just gone through the loss of their own dog, Rocky.

Karrie's younger sister Kathy and her three children met us at the house to say their last goodbyes. Lacey was not strong enough to stand on her own, so my brother-in-law, Jerry and his daughter Rachel carried Lacey out to the van on her bed. Janaye, who had always wanted Lacey to live with them, came down to say a teary goodbye along with the other kids. We then got Lacey settled in and Becca climbed in the back seat to keep watch over her on the ride home. There they were, Arby and Lacey, nose to nose, the young and the old—the contrast of the brown-eyed, light yellow Lab, youthful and still at the beginning of his life, and the dark soulful-eyed, black corporate lady, seasoned in her journey, waiting to go home. She lay there

Arby and Lacey hanging out.

on the side of the van where she had ridden hundreds of times over hundreds of miles for over ten years of her life.

As we traveled home (a 4-½ hour trip), we decided we should stop and allow Lacey to stretch her legs and get some fresh air. We chose a nice rest stop outside of Moses Lake, then carried Lacey on her bed out of the van and set her on the cool grass. After sitting there for a moment, she got up on shaky legs and I took her by the leash and encouraged her by saying what I had said a thousand times before: "Do your business, Lacey."

She surprised us all by walking slowly eight times in a circle around me, just as she had done for years. When she was done, she walked back over to her bed and lay down, almost as if to say, "I'm ready, let's go!" We carried her back to the van, made sure she was comfortable and continued home to Bellevue.

Once home, we lifted Lacey out of the van and placed her on the grass. She proceeded to get up and walk in her circles around me again just as she had for all of those years. Just as Karrie and I were ready to place her back on her bed, she started moving toward the house on her own. Now the front of our house has two steps—Lacey managed to walk up the steps and inside as if to say, "I remember this." We gave her some soft food and she again surprised us by eating all of it, then looked at me as if to say, "A little more, please." After drinking a little water, she lay down on the floor next to Arby and fell asleep. Karrie took the first watch of the night—when I came down at 3 a.m. to relieve her, Karrie reported Lacey had slept well for most of the early part of the night. She had gotten a little restless and had started pacing so Karrie took her outside. Again, down the stairs she went, then back up the stairs with a little hop to get her rear end up the steps and went back to bed.

In the morning, Becca got up not wanting to go to school; she had grown up with Lacey by her side and the thought of not seeing her again was breaking her heart. Not knowing what the day would bring, we all agreed that she would go to school, taking Karrie's phone to check in with us or for us to communicate with her when we knew what the plan was going to be for Lacey. Then we took a moment to call Jacob who was away at college to let him know what was happening. We wanted to give him the chance to come home and say goodbye. As much as he wanted to see her again, he knew it would take time for him to get home and he did not want Lacey to be in pain or to prolong the inevitable. He loved her too much to do that.

Arby keeps watch over Lacey on the last night

Before taking Lacey outside, I gave her some more food and she ate as much that morning as she had eaten the night before. After eating, I walked her outside and again she navigated the stairs fairly well. After taking care of things outside she walked back into the house, lay down and looked at me like "What's the big deal?" Karrie and I sat trying to enjoy our coffee and not thinking about the day ahead of us.

After an hour or so, we decided it was time to go to the veterinarian's office. Karrie had walked Lacey out to the van. I looked at Karrie and said, "Okay, how we are going to get her in?" We opened the slider and before we knew it, Lacey hopped in just like she had done for over 10 years. The difference this time was that only the front end went in. She looked over her shoulder as if to say, "A little help here, please!" So Karrie lifted up Lacey's rear legs and helped her in.

As we drove the short distance, I thought about what the veterinarian would tell us. What decision would we have to make? How much longer would Lacey be with us? Could I have two dogs in the house? What would be best for both Lacey and Arby? How will this affect me? You see, even though this was my fourth working guide, I had never gone full circle with any of them. Usually the dog had been career-changed or had retired—that dog would then be with another family and I would not be there. However, Lacey was different. She was the first guide dog that I ever had with a wife and children. When she retired, Lacey went to live with our family in Idaho and we would see her every time we would go and visit them ... now here we were, traveling to the veterinarian to have her evaluated to determine what the next step should be and I just did not know what that was.

Arby and Lacey - 2010

At the Newport Animal Hospital, Karrie and I helped Lacey out of the car and into the waiting room. As we stepped in, Karrie started to tell the person behind the counter that we were here and that Dr. Brown was expecting us. As she began to speak, her words choked from the upwelling of emotion as the tears began and the realization of the possible events hit. They escorted us into one of the rooms that Lacey and Arby had both been in many times over the years. We sat down on the floor next to Lacey who was lying down on a little rug to be comfortable and stay warm. She put her head close to my legs and I began petting her and talking to her. Karrie took pictures of us and the three of us just sat together on that floor loving on each other, remembering how wonderful the years had been.

When Dr. Brown came in, she got down on the floor with Lacey and carefully began the examination. After a few moments she let us know that Lacey was suffering from the normal hip challenges of old age, incontinence, inability to eat, her teeth were not doing well, and her stomach was tender to the touch. She told us that, yes, Lacey was in pain but hiding it well. She had the beginning stages of stomach cancer and that to prolong her life would not be in her best interest. She offered to make Lacey more comfortable to give her more time with us—more days, perhaps even weeks—but she was also very honest and told us that Lacey would be in pain and would continue to get worse. Dr. Brown left the room to allow us to talk things over.

As we talked, Karrie said that Lacey looked content. We realized that in the last twenty-four hours, Lacey had, in many ways, found a second wind— eating, drinking, walking, coming home and sleeping next to Arby, getting up and down stairs and even getting in the car (almost) by herself. She had come full circle and had been strong to the very end. It was a good time to say goodbye. We let Dr. Brown know that we were ready; she came in and told us that she would be administering a shot to Lacey, that she would feel no pain and it would take effect in a very short time span. After she gave the injection, Dr. Brown left the room and Karrie and I sat there with Lacey. I had tears running down my cheeks as I stroked her head, talking to her and telling her, "Thank you for being my companion and friend for all of these years." I told her it was okay to go and that she would be running through the fields with Rocky, playing and being young again. Her breathing became very quiet and then stopped altogether. Neither of us wanted to leave, neither of us could believe she was gone; we just sat there on the cold linoleum floor, the warmth of Lacey on our laps. The only sound in the room was that of Karrie and I crying; a hushed silence, a quiet choked sob, a whisper to my beautiful corporate lady, a feeling of peace.

As we drove away, I called the family to tell them that she was now resting peacefully, no longer in pain, running in the fields with Rocky...but as I started talking I lost it emotionally—the words would not come. I did not expect this as I had thought I was fine. I knew it was the right decision, but it hit me hard. My friend, trusted companion, guide dog and family pet had passed.

I thank you, my beautiful dark-eyed, corporate lady for keeping me safe for ten wonderful years. You helped to give me the confidence to go out and live life to its fullest. Thank you, Guide Dogs, for the incredible job you do as you breed these animals and place them with puppy raisers for the first part of their life, then walk in the shadows—always there to support until the end.

Thank you to the Morimoto family for giving Lacey her start and the ability to travel and interact with people. She was well trained and she used that daily in our lives together. To all Puppy Raisers, you give a gift that is priceless—the love you pour into your Guide Puppies in training overflows into each of our lives when we receive our Guide Dog.

And finally, to my incredible family in Spokane—thank you for loving Lacey and caring for her during her final years. This journey that God has us on is made possible by your love and your support. Thank you for helping Lacey to come full circle.

Lacey, My Corporate Lady
4/15/97 - 5/14/12

CHAPTER TWELVE

Testimonies

Clark Roberts has encouraged and motivated thousands of people to live a life that is full; to realize that each of us has gifts, talents and abilities and that we can each make a difference; to learn that a person can live their life in a way that helps others to live their life in a new way.

See what people of all ages are saying:

Dear Clark Roberts,

Thank you for your wonderful and interesting guest speaker presentation. "You have been a great example to show us how we should persevere in life. We have guest speakers because it makes it so we all know what we could do in the future and how we could deal with conflicts when we're older.

Seeing you speak during class made me realize how we could take care of any obstacles that life may throw at us. Knowing that such a person like you can overcome being blind by still doing and achieving things you have always loved. You are an inspiration, and I'm thankful that you came in to speak.

Sincerely, Zoe — 7th grade

Dear Mr. Roberts,

Thank you for coming into our AVID class. Thank you for teaching all of us that if you believe you can achieve something, you will have the ability to do it. This relates to AVID because it stands for Advancement Via Individual Determination. We learn about not giving up and trying to do new things. We have all sorts of guest speakers. This is because it shows us that everyone has potential to do what they want in life.

One thing I learned from you is that you had a life-changing thing that happened to you and you still do the things you love. This makes me want to keep doing what I want when something big changes in my life. One question I still have is, "Do you ever think about your life before you lost your sight?" Anyways, thank you very much for taking your time to drop by our class.

Sincerely, Leon — 8th grade

Dear Clark Roberts,

Thank you for coming in. It really has made me see things differently to see someone that lost their eyesight be living such a great life and being very happy and still be able to do many of the things they normally did before the blindness. I'm Christian, I'm thirteen, I just have glasses and I don't like it— but you're blind and you have a great life. It was very important for you to come to show that if someone wants to do something they can, and no one has any excuses. You're blind and that hasn't held you back, so there's nothing that can hold us back from getting a great education.

I learned so many things from you like you should appreciate everything you have and use it to its full capacity. That even if you lose something important like your eyes, you shouldn't worry about what you lost but be grateful for what you still have. I have one question for you, "What got you through such a hard time?" Once again, thank you for coming in.

Sincerely, Christian — 7th grade

Mr. Roberts spoke to our third, fourth, and fifth graders about perseverance, courage, and honor, and to never give up no matter what the challenge. During his talk, Mr. Roberts had captivated all age groups, prompting many very wonderful questions of curiosity.

It is very clear Mr. Roberts has the ability to help our young and young adults be aware of an ability we all hold whether we are disabled or not.

Kitty Chadwick —Counselor, Skyway Elementary.
Coeur d'Alene, Idaho

Clark is good at keeping a vision alive inside of himself and sharing hope for others to do the same. He lets you know that you can succeed.

Karla Busenbark — A.V.I.D. teacher,
Chinook Middle School, Bellevue, WA

Clark's message and approach to the students gave them a sense of strength and hope that they can make a difference in their futures.

Chris Hammons — Principal,
Lakes Magnet (Middle) School,
Coeur d'Alene, ID

Clark Roberts demonstrates celebrating differences, helping students recognize challenges as growth opportunities, and supporting students to take on their challenges as personal growth objectives.

...Clark has a compelling story and can share his emotions as well as the struggles he encountered moving from a life of sight to a life of blindness. His story, and his willingness to share it, helps students put their own day-to-day challenges into perspective.

Judy Buckmaster — Principal,
Tyee Middle School, Bellevue, WA

Loren Reynolds — Professor, Everett Community College

Dear Clark,

Hi, my name is Erin, and I just wanted to thank you for coming in and speaking in my Communications class! Your story made me realize that I am going to start trusting more people in my life. You also made me realize that only I hold myself back from enjoying life. That life is too short, so to enjoy every minute. I came to my Communications class today not knowing what to expect; we were just told us that we were having a guest that would be discussing his perception on life. I wanted to come to hear what you had to say. You have shown me that, if I want to, I can achieve whatever I want even with the biggest setbacks! I enjoyed hearing your story it was truly inspiring and thank you so much for your time!

Erin — Student at Everett Community College

Dear Clark,

Our Instructor told us that there was a visitor coming to talk to us to give us his perception and perspective on life. You asked what I have learned. I have learned to appreciate myself and thank God for every day I live— Overcome fears —Anything in life can be overcome. The definition of TRUST: (Teamwork, Recreation, Uncertainties, Support, To rely upon someone or something totally).

I came to know about guide animals, and had never seen them before. What is going to be different from what I have learned today? I am going to respect everyone and not stereotype people with disabilities and know that anything in life can happen and change a person's life forever. I became stronger than ever, if a person with disability can be strong then why can't I? To trust in myself and know that I can do anything and to believe that people with disability can also be independent

Thank you so much for your explanation.

Florence Luk — Student, Everett Community College

This man spoke about the life lessons that he has learned through the tragedy of losing his sight. He and his guide dog clearly illustrated the concept of trust in a spellbinding presentation. You could literally hear a pin drop in the auditorium as Clark told his story! After his talk, students were able to come up and ask questions. They left inspired by this man's warmth and positive approach to life.

Sincerely, Dave Jennings — Middle School Principal,
Northwest Christian School

It is my pleasure to highly recommend Mr. Clark Roberts as an excellent speaker for any school setting from Kindergarten to High School. Mr. Roberts (helped by his dog "Arby") shared the difficulty of becoming blind at an early age and how he overcame this trial to live a joyful and vibrant life. This chapel resulted in some amazing classroom discussions, where many students came to the understanding that life challenges can result in amazing future blessings.

One of our teachers at the elementary school said it best:
What an inspirational chapel to have Clark Roberts as our guest speaker! He and Mr. Arbuckle make a great team. The students were fascinated with a guide dog at first, but soon we were hearing a powerful testimony of God at work in a man's life to "work everything together for good." We could almost feel his pain at 18 years of age as he described the devastating news of his coming vision loss. Hard things do happen to good people, but how inspiring to hear a personal story of a life surrendered to Christ and how God can use it to draw us closer to Him and to challenge and comfort others who may also face struggles and hardships in life. Mr. Roberts lives life to the fullest and doesn't let his blindness rob him of joy. He has great humor and fun adventures to tell about, as well as sharing how he must trust others daily: his dog, other people, and especially the Lord. We, too, can remember the scripture ten-word prayer, "I can do all things through Christ who strengthens me." I hope we can have Mr. Roberts back again and I would highly recommend him to other schools.

Mrs. Kathy Donahoe — 1ˢᵗ grade Teacher

...Additionally, one of our students, David, who was born with significant birth defects, was profoundly impacted by Mr. Robert's life story. It gave this young man, who will have a lifetime of physical limitations, the ability to view his disabilities as an opportunity for growth. I am profoundly thankful to Mr. Roberts for helping this young man look at his weakness as his greatest strength.

It is evident that Mr. Roberts lives for the glory of God and the encouragement of everyone he meets. He is a powerful testimony to the power of God to transform any situation or difficulty for our good and His glory. I, as well as the entire student body, can't wait to have him back next year!

Terry Meyer — Elementary Principal,
Northwest Christian Schools

ACKNOWLEDGMENTS

To my Lord and Savior, Jesus Christ, for knowing I was strong enough to receive the "gift" of blindness. My parents, Elva and Lewis Roberts, gave me real-life training on how to accept challenges and live with uncertainties; to realize that when life hits you hard, quitting is not an option. I know they are smiling in Heaven as they watch over me daily. I love and miss you, Mom and Dad.

> *Trust in the Lord with all of your heart, and lean not on your*
> *own understanding. In all your ways acknowledge Him, and*
> *He will make your paths straight.* ~ *Proverbs 3: 5-6 (NIV)*

The above scripture was given to me by my mother when I graduated from high school-little did she know how this verse would become my cornerstone.

To my wife Karrie, thank you for your support and encouragement and the countless hours working and reworking my stories. Your enthusiasm, energy, unconditional love and patience are a blessing to me. You have always been and continue to be my beautiful butterfly. Without you, this book would not be a reality. To Jacob and Becca, I will never forget how I would tell you the stories of growing up, stories about my guide dogs and the fun we used to have, and how when I was done you would ask me to tell you another story. These stories are for you. Your love for me and your total acceptance of my sight loss blesses me every day.

Deep gratitude is given to Stephen Dennis—for without your no-holds-barred honesty and encouragement to dig deep, this book and its stories would not truly reflect my heart and emotions. In true fashion, God intervened at just the right time and sent us our copy and technical editing angel, Fran Lee. Fran, this book would not have made it to the finish line without your gift of editing, determination, and copious attention to detail.

To Elliott Wolf of Peanut Butter Publishing, thank you for your guidance and willingness to share your wisdom. To Bruce Hudson of Hudson's Portrait Designs for his friendship and amazing gift of photography; my friends from Dog About Town, the Christmas at the Lake shop (a special wag goes out to Mika), The Museum of Flight, and so many others that have encouraged me to write and dream beyond the limits of my sight loss.

Thank you to Guide Dogs for the Blind and to Puppy Raisers everywhere. Without you, there would have not been five guide dogs and all of the stories and memories that came over the span of 30 years. Your organization is truly a gift and a blessing that has made this possible.

To my family and friends who keep me laughing, keep me humble, and help to create a place in my life that I love to be. They are my reminder that life is full, life is humorous, and life is a gift!

Clark, Karrie, Becca and Jacob—and, of course, Arby

To book a presentation by Clark for your business, school, church or youth group, email Clark at ultimatevision@live.com. You can also find information on www.Ultimate-Vision.org or at Facebook under www.facebook.com/clarkrobertsultimatevision.

Additional Resources:
Internet Podcast – K9sportskonnections *interview with Clark Roberts*
www.wagstoyou.blogspot.com - Arby's Blog
www.guidedogs.com – Guide Dogs for the Blind website
Harnessing the Power of Partnership – Guide Dogs for the Blind informational YouTube clip